I AM YOU

One soul two bodies

I AM YOU

One soul two bodies

A TRUE LOVE STORY

BY
SEACOMBE

T

Illustrations by Mark Huntley & Howard Flanagan
Cover design by Beth Walker

The manufacturer's authorised representative in the EU for product safety is
Authorised Rep Compliance Ltd, 71 Lower Baggot Street,
Dublin D02 P593 Ireland (www.arccompliance.com).

Troubador Publishing Ltd
Unit E2 Airfield Business Park
Harrison Road, Market Harborough
Leicestershire LE16 7UL
Tel: 0116 279 2299
Email: books@troubador.co.uk
Web: www.troubador.co.uk

ISBN 978 1806341 047

British Library Cataloguing in Publication Data.
A catalogue record for this book is available from the British Library.

Printed and bound in the UK by TJ Books, Padstow, Cornwall
Typeset in 10pt Minion Pro by Troubador Publishing Ltd, Leicester, UK

'for whatever we lose (like a you or a me)
it's only ourselves we find in the sea'
(E. E. Cummings 1894–1962)

Contents

This book is dedicated to
my twin Julia

'To divide is not to take away'
(P. B. Shelley 1772–1822)

Foreword

I AM YOU is a true story *of the innocence of the ultimate love connection.*

Many people may well have experienced for themselves, a connection with another individual in their lifetime. A resonance and comfort that feels soothing and easy, where everything is somehow so 'second nature'. The term 'soul mate' is often used to describe such a bond.

However, it is widely understood there is an even greater and deeper spiritual soul experience – and it is regarded as *the most intense* soul connection two individuals can ever encounter. It is an explosion of pure unfiltered love and is the ultimate passionate experience of soul intimacy where incredible magnetism and the need to be connected abounds – *non-stop.* Termed *Mirror-Souls* or *Twin-Flames* the soul instantly recognises their other created half – their soul twin from many past lives together. Once reunited, the bond is binding and unbreakable. One can never choose to meet their Twin-Flame, not many do, but the events that unfold after the initial recognition are beyond control.

The relationship – often traumatic – may upset societal norms and traditions, creating new ways of thinking and understanding about Love, by re-shaping existing boundaries along the way. It is an intense, passionate love reunion in the pursuit of oneness between two individuals of the same vibrational frequency where every sensation is ecstatically and agonisingly amplified.

I AM YOU is the true tale of such a love reunion experienced at the time and without any knowledge or understanding of Twin-Flames. The story is told in this innocence.

Set in Dorset on and around the Isle of Purbeck and the Jurassic Coast, it is the warm summer of 2004. Only character names, certain place names and the timeline have been altered.

Seacombe, 2025

'And when one of them meets his other half, the actual half of himself, the pair are lost in an amazement of love and friendship and intimacy and one will not be out of sight of the other even for a moment'

(Plato 427–348 BC)

From
The Journals of George J. Seacombe

Friday August 13th

To:
Mr G. Seacombe
'Greenground'
Bere Regis
Dorset

Memories of our yesterday…

A thin, late summer breeze, willow trees dipping their leaves, cool greens, graceful swallows and blue dragonfly. Wings over water rings. A seat of perfect peace where cool afternoon shadows fell upon the tall-reeded bank of the Wareham River.

With the warm hand of summer reassuringly on our naked backs and my love's eyes looking deeply into mine, I wondered, how-can-this-ever-be-surpassed?

Again, please… (v. soon)

Your love

x

Four Months Previously

May 2004

'Welcome Back!'

Sunday 23rd May

10:45
Bedroom Olympics: ↓
Work forecast: ↑

It's a lazy late Sunday morning. The summer sun is streaming in through the half-opened bedroom window onto worn white cotton bed sheets and naked flesh. A much-ruffled duvet lies bundled to one end of the bed, and I rest with the sun on my face and enjoy a light gust of fresh Dorset breeze that whooshes in through my favourite view.

I have the once crisp and neat Sunday papers scattered over the bedroom floor while Lois is downstairs making fresh coffee.

She shouts up the stairs, somewhat cheekily, 'You recovered yet? Brew is on its way.'

'Er, yes,' I grunt. 'Are you making any toast? There's some soda bread and homemade jam in the cupboard.'

'Okay. Bloody pauper's food on its way then. Five minutes!'

I turn my head towards the window and move a fraction to gain the full force of the sunlight on my face and inhale the fresh clean air. It is going to be a lovely day again.

The sound of bare feet climbing the stairs resonates up the narrow hallway, then there is an ominous *clang* followed by, 'Shit, shit, shit! Spilt some coffee on the carpet. Two minutes!'

Five minutes later, Lois and her body are back in the bedroom. 'Sorry about that, tray was wider than the corner of those stairs. I blame the owner for lack of foresight.'

'Those tight stairs are part of the character of the house. I would never change them. It's why the furniture up here is so bijou and self-assembled! Getting this bed up here was a masterpiece of engineering, I can tell you. It took three of us to manoeuvre the pieces around those tight corners and amazingly I only had to remove one door surround, but it was millimetre tight.'

'The bed is good, definitely worth all that effort and this view out the window is incredible. To be able to lie in bed and wake to that each day is such a treat.' She brushes a stray hair away from my forehead. 'But you already know that, don't you?'

I flip her over in one move to face the window and hold her firmly around her waist with one arm, and we take in the view as one.

'Yup, I most certainly do – and I never, ever take it for granted.'

The vista from my bedroom window, and from the sitting room window downstairs, was the reason for purchasing the cottage in the first place. There's a one-kilometre uninterrupted view across lush green lark-filled downland that leads to the rolling curves of a tall Neolithic chalk hill that looks much like a dozing giant. Everything I can see changes hue during the day as the sunlight wraps the hillside into shadow and produces every possible shade of green – from rich, bright malachite to a dark, moody olive. Throughout the year the hill is an entertainment in itself with a countenance that is always changing. Each morning when I wake up, I tilt my head to one side, peer from the pillow through the mullioned window and say to myself, *What's the hill up to?* In much the same way, whenever I pass over a bridge and look down at a river below or drive along by the shore and look at the sea, it's always *What's the water up to?*

'What are we going to do for a holiday this summer, then?' Lois asks, out of the blue. 'I feel we need to sort one out soon.'

'Eh? You're off to Greece in a couple of weeks if I'm not mistaken. Deserting me.'

'True, but I am supposed to be sort of working, helping out at a beach bar and all that, so it doesn't really count. I mean a *real* holiday.'

'Oh, I see, a *real* holiday. Well, Dorset is pretty good for that, you know.'

'Yes, yes, c'mon, somewhere where the weather is guaranteed hot and the waters are wonderfully warm. Lovely as it is here, you just can't bank on the British weather. Look at last summer, it pretty well rained all of July and August.'

'How do you know? You weren't here for most of it!'

'Well, I read about it in the *Montana Gazette*!'

'Yeah, you bloody defector. Anyway, I'll do a bit of research on my posh new iMac and have a ponder, see what's out there for us. But you do know I have a few big races on this year and I'd really like to do well in them.'

'You're truly mad, you know that. When will you realise you're no longer the super swimmer you once were. You're forty-two years old now and the winning days of your youth are long gone. You can't keep pushing yourself and driving your body expecting to win.'

'The water has no idea of age. Besides, I love my swimming… and also my kayaking… and my cycling. It's in me. It's the competitive thing. I adore the water and I love those Dorset hills and I simply love racing. It's important and it's what I do.'

'Yes, I do understand, I think, it is *part* of your appeal after all… plus it does give you… a rather nice…'

Lois twists herself round to face me, then – with the alacrity of a gymnast – straddles my thighs.

'A nice what?' I enquire.

'Umm, a rather nice…'

She lowers herself forward, then kisses the top of my chest, then the top of my stomach muscles before working her way down lower and lower at a teasingly seductive pace.

'Umm… a bod,' she says purringly, 'a bod for me to play with and whittle away *the rest of the day*!'

'Ah. Okay, then,' I feign, pathetically. 'If you *really insist*…'

Monday 24th May

09:30
Blue Dorset sky F3-4, SW, +23°
Office forecast: ↑
Training: ↑

Lois is tidying up her things and making a few phone calls before she makes the long drive back to her home in Sussex, so I've left her to get on with it at the cottage. In the meantime, and before I put my work head on, I thought I'd grab some quiet pool time to myself. Put in some steady training by ploughing up and down an empty swimming lane.

There is nothing quite like the feeling of stretching out in the water in a lane all to yourself. Maintaining a long slow relaxed stroke, fixing on a piece of water with your hand and then levering over the top of it, feeling the sensation on the skin as the water parts its solidity and generously allows you in – as if permission has been granted by a higher authority who's said, 'Yup, you can come through, but only because you appreciate it.' The sensation is even more pronounced when the water temperature is low, then every movement in pursuit of efficiency is sensed by receptor cells, emphasising the motion, sending signals and status reports back to the brain until it, in turn, is numbed by the cold and thereafter confusion reigns.

That's why, personally, I don't do cold water voluntarily. Too many close shaves with hypothermia. But in the pool, the sensation of being immersed – particularly in clear undisturbed haze-free water – as if it is the purest clean waters of the Mediterranean or Caribbean, where marine life can be as inquisitive as its guest, is compelling enough to warrant multiple re-visits. And more some. Well it is in my case.

I spend most of my swimming time not actually in the water but somewhere else. I know not where. Sometimes it is a place as mundane as floating above my office desk worrying about the next business move, other times, my dreamland is more exotic and I'm an aquanaut beneath the ocean discovering new sea life. A place where sensations abound with every available hue of blueness; and sensations of speed, lots of speed, lots of nimble otter-like slinky movements. A place that is friendly, kind, tolerant and warm, warm to the core, warm to the very delicate fringes of the soul.

I check the pool's Speedo timing clock; it's about to hit the 'red top', so I push off from the wall, toes immediately pointed, feet as flat as my dodgy ankles will allow, my arms stretched out in front of me, my hands and fingers clasped one on top of the other – left over right – and my head lodged between my biceps, face looking down to the dappled mosaic tiles of the pool bottom. I try to imagine I'm as streamlined as a porpoise with a purpose.

I surface twelve metres or so down the pool, turn my head a fraction to the right and suck in some air quickly before placing it back into the water, and get my arms into action – firstly pulling through with my left hand and then spearing the water with my right hand, grabbing something 'solid' then quickly pulling it through alongside my body. I rotate to the left this time to take in some air, think about my streamlined feet, and then pierce the water with my left hand and move forward through the water as efficiently as I can manage, minimising any drag while maximising the effort of the pull with my hands and arms. It all happens so quickly and before I can think about anything else, the end wall suddenly appears and it is time for a tumble turn. *Come in straight, focus on the tumble and push off hard* I say to myself, *streamline your body* and I put in a dolphin kick to help keep up my momentum.

I clear twelve metres underwater again, then grab some air and start pulling through with my arms, fixing on the water with my hands and levering myself through. Again, before I've had enough time to think about my stroke the wall is there and it's tumble time once again, but now I check the timing clock for my fifty-metre split, and it's showing an okay time. Can I hold this pace for another fifty metres, or will I start tying-up as the lactic acid starts forming in the muscles? I suck in more air and midway down the third length I begin to breathe every other arm stroke as opposed to every four as my need for oxygen increases. I hit the wall for the last tumble turn and think it is the best yet; with two dolphin kicks underwater, which propels me a good distance down the pool, I dig in hard pulling with all the strength I can muster and feel the muscles of my thighs, chest, lats and forearms begin to burn. I'm grimacing. My mouth is wide open underwater like a whale shark about to feed and I hang on for a few more metres, sighting the end wall and willing it to arrive as easily as it did just a lap before. I reach for the tiles. My right hand touches and I glance up from the surface of the water and check my time.

Phew! I'm breathing heavily, deep long breaths, and my heart is thumping so much it is reverberating through my ribcage. It's a 1:07 and that's okay, but can I do another one like that with just forty-five seconds' rest? I ponder for a few seconds and think it's worth a go, so I wait for the next 'red top' and set off once again on a 100-metre lope. Now I wish I wasn't swimming alone.

I come to the first turn, flip over as before and hit the sweet spot. This one feels good, and I glide underwater a satisfactory distance and emerge on the surface like Red October being chased from the deeps. I gasp for air and continue to pull through at a comfortable pace, stretching my arms out even further, trying to glide a little more while putting in more effort with my leg kick. The wall appears again and I push off, but this time I feel a familiar tell-tale sensation of a drained feeling down the legs. It starts at the top of the thighs and flows towards the calf muscles, as if a tap has been opened from the soles of your feet and all one's strength is rapidly pouring out, like blood from a wound. *I'm not going to keep this pace up*, I say to myself, and consciously throttle back, knowing that the last tumble turn will be a disaster if I don't take in some more oxygen in the next few strokes. The wall arrives; I know it is slower and I glance up at the clock. Yup, 1:10. I've dropped three seconds.

What can I blame? Who can I blame? I need an excuse and I need it now! These irrational thoughts flood my brain in a millisecond of seeing the clock, as if I *have to have* a reason for the slower time and can't believe that perhaps I'm just not fit enough to maintain that pace. I sink back down under the water and push off from the wall, but this time on backstroke and set off slowly on a few recovery lengths, staring at the glass roof canopy and still questioning why I could not hold my pace. I find solace in the thought that had my swim club chums been in the water with me, I would have perhaps gone a little faster – and with that pathetic fillip, I flip back over onto my front and continue to crack on with the rest of my session and my aquatic world.

14:45

I arrive home and Lois has loaded her car and looks ready to depart.

'Had enough, then?'

'No, not really, but I should be heading back. I've another job that starts this week and I really need to sort things out for that.'

'Uh-huh, I understand. Okay, I must get on too I suppose. I've a PowerPoint presentation to finish for an important meeting this Wednesday.'

'Well, the very best of luck with that. I'm sure you'll land a deal. They'll love your range of eco products and what you've created. Going green, it's definitely the future.'

'I have to believe so,' I say, trying to buoy myself up a bit.

'Of course, you must.'

I walk her to the car, we embrace, kiss one another on both cheeks and I wave her goodbye. She disappears off along the lane in a cloud of dust, tooting her air horn as she goes. In just a few seconds she has turned the corner and is out of view.

THREE DAYS LATER

Thursday 27th May

19:30
Some blue F2-3, E, +16°
Exercise: Revelatory!
Work forecast: ⟵⟶

Swim training session.

Cantankerous lane 2 are squabbling again and there's a great deal of chatter. Swim coach Mark notices and walks over and says, 'Will you lot stop acting like a bunch of annoying little schoolchildren. Sort yourselves out. There's too many in this swim lane – you, you and you move to lanes 1 and 3.'

There's more commotion, laughter and jibes as the lane thins out and the session is ready to start. Mark barks out the swim-set: 'Two hundred warm-up, followed by eight fifties kick.' There are a few boos. Not everyone likes kicking, particularly the triathletes who generally compete in a wetsuit where a strong leg kick is not really required and for whom kicking is just a pointless and painful chore.

I've been standing in the water at the end of the lane with four others while all this has been going on like a goody-two-shoes, with my back facing down the pool and half submerged.

Through the misty confines of my goggles I notice someone elegantly sliding in from the poolside. *Er, who's this?* I say to myself. *Wow, nice figure*, but before I can appreciate matters further, I am tapped on my shoulder to get the lane underway and I turn around, slip under the water and begin to head down the pool.

It's nice to get going. There's always an enlivening caress of cool water that runs down your skin when you first get moving, as if the tyre warmers have been quickly taken off a racing car and it is the first lap of the circuit. It kickstarts the body – a call to action – although it fades promptly enough. By the end of the first length, all temperatures are up and in the green.

As I head back down, I notice the new-person-in-the-lane has gone off last but is already on Rob's toes. *Interesting*, I say to myself, *probably over-eager*. I carry on with the warm-up at a steady pace. On the final length, I see she's breaststroking behind him; a sure sign that she is being held up. I stop at the lane end and grab a kick float. I wait for the others to finish before setting off on the eight two-length kick. Kicking is not a strong point of mine at all; with a bit of cheating and a chunk of rest between each set I can usually just about hang on at the front, but I'm more than happy for anyone else to lead the lane should they wish. Girls are normally better than boys at kicking – something to do with flexibility, I think – and I turn to the new-vision-in-the-lane, who is barely breathing and already smiling.

'Would you like to lead this part?' I ask.

'I couldn't possibly,' she replies politely.

'No, no, you can, really, please don't hold back!'

'I am happy here, honestly. But thank you,' she says, ever so more politely and very beautifully.

I set off, kickboard in my outstretched hands and my legs thumping out some sort of forward propulsion, but my head is beginning to sputter erratically. *Who, what, who, is this person?* I'm weirdly over-intrigued. While I swim, there are a variety of questions buzzing wildly around my head, crashing into each other like a dozen drunken Tinkerbells high on amphetamines. *Who is she?*

I watch her come down the lane as I'm heading back up and see she's not really trying while making it all look very easy. I feign a lack of interest and, as we pass, adopt a pained, effortful grimace I believe would fool the harshest film critic. The set continues, and on the last length I decide to place my head to one side, making it easier to look at this new vision directly. *My God, she is beautiful*. I smile broadly and it works. She beams right back at me and I feel an uncontainable surge of elation. I'm chuffed to bits with myself and stand proudly at the shallow end as if I've just won a big race and am enjoying the applause. Instead, swim coach Mark barks out the main set while looking directly down at me. It has the rapid effect of bringing me back down to earth.

I listen to what he says and then eagerly turn around to see what *The Vision* is doing, and notice she's looking up at the timing clock.

This gives me, for the briefest moment, an opportunity to look at her unashamedly, and I am lost to this world. *She is very beautiful indeed*. I notice, however, that her goggles are so heavily tinted I am unable to see her eyes, so I quickly drop my gaze, fearful she may be looking directly back at me. Argh!

The main swim-set starts and I'm leading the lane again, which requires my full concentration to keep the pace high and for us to hit the target times. In the middle of each length, though, through the bubbles and swirls of freneticism,

I try to monitor where she is and absorb all too briefly her Marina-like shape underwater. I wonder, *what colour are her eyes? What colour is her hair?* There are no clues; there are no obvious giveaways whatsoever.

The session cracks on and I'm willing it to end, or at least to take a short break so I can sneak a few more glances towards her. *Who is she? What sort of age is she? Late twenties, early thirties possibly? What's her name? Will she ever come back again?* Time seems to drag.

Eventually, the warm-down arrives and I'm relieved that the pace slows. Perhaps now I can summon up the courage and find a moment to speak to her. Somewhat annoyingly, she is already in conversation with swim-friend Brent. I slide up slowly to where they are standing, noticing she's still got her goggles and cap on, but try to get a more detailed look. Even more annoyingly, just as I get within a couple of metres, Dave distracts me and calls me over from the next lane and begins telling me about an upcoming race and the finer details of the travel arrangements. I'm not at all interested. By the time he's finished waffling, I can see Brent is now standing on his own and quickly I scan around the poolside, but I can't see *The Vision* anywhere.

'What did you say that scared her off so quickly?' I say to him.

He laughs. 'No, mate, she was just telling me she had to shoot as it's nearly her children's bedtime.'

'Eh, really. Wow! Children! Er, is she going to join the club, do you know?'

'Dunno, mate. Probably.'

My spirits lifted somewhat by the word *probably*, I head to the changing room animated from head to toe. It's all very irrational for my brain to comprehend. Too many questions buzzing around my head, but I'm excited.

Friday 28th May

11:20
Blue bits F1-2, SW, +21°
Training: ←→
Work forecast: Mixed

Another cup of coffee: the third this morning and each has been stronger than the last. They're feeding my headache in some unconsciously-sought-after sadomasochistic manner. It's as if pain will help divert my thoughts from That Woman. Note the phraseology. Last night she was a vision, a goddess and sight to behold. Now, after too little sleep, I'm annoyed at the disturbed state of my mind. Made fitful. So, today, she's very much 'That Woman'. But what is it about her that has so rudely garnered my attention? That voice of hers, it's so soothing.

12:30
This is by no means normal behaviour. Absolutely not.

13:30
Work action plan: Fax business partner Graham the details of two small orders and the updated customer information. Fix the goddamn printer.

14:40
What's the likelihood 'That Woman/The Vision' will be at swim training tomorrow morning?

15:15
Work action: Get new product label designs off to the printers ASAP. Order up more sales brochures.

15:30
Polish lenses on swim goggles. Try on new pair of swim jammers.

16:15
Action: Chase up a new exciting sales enquiry and put another call into Graham.

17:00
Try on those tight jammers again. Check look in mirror. Iron swim towel.

Saturday 29th May

08:00
Blue still F2-3, SW, +24°
Training: ↑
Work forecast: ↑

Morning training is about to start. I'm in the water and cruising – doing a moderately paced breaststroke while the lane fills up with late arrivals. No sign of 'The Vision' so far. Perhaps Thursday nights are the only time she can swim? One part of me is relieved, the other is profoundly disappointed. I tell myself to stop being concerned about someone I know nothing about, to enjoy the water and the company of my swim-friends as I do most Saturday mornings.

It works, and for the first few lengths I am back in the familiar zone of pain and physical pleasure as I plough up and down the pool as fast as I can, trying to catch those ahead and not be caught by those behind. But then I notice a shape in the water that is somehow already heart-achingly familiar. She's here. My stomach is in turmoil. Instantly, butterflies perform their own Cirque Du Soleil. *Now, what do I do?*

Last night, I had repeatedly played out this scenario in my head, this and about five other variations. Each one ended up with me remaining calm, mature, sophisticated and in control. Now though, even the water, my best friend and defender of worldly incursions, feels unfamiliar. Suddenly, it has an altogether different and strange texture. The world has truly turned on its axis.

I adopt a Zen-like poise and smile serenely at all and sundry as the lane gathers together and we wait for the session to start. She's wearing those dark goggles again and I wonder, in a moment of peculiar defensive self-importance, whether she has noticed I have a new pair of jammers on. She smiles at me. In an instant my inner turmoil is soothed, and the colour of the water returns to its normal happy shade of becalming blue.

The session rolls on. I try to grab the opportunity to say something between set rests, but every time I make an attempt someone else gets in there first.

I take time out and watch her swim effortlessly and confidently up and down the lane. Through clear or even misted goggles, I can see she is entirely at home in my environment. She moves sublimely with all the flowing grace of one born to the water.

The whistle blows and the hour-long session comes to a close. I make sure I'm at the shallow end early this time, in the hope of being able to say something, anything, before she exits the water and disappears away.

I sidle over to the corner of the pool where she's standing and go for it. 'Well, you certainly don't need any swimming lessons, do you?' I say, very clumsily. But it works! With one foot already on the poolside steps, she slides gracefully back down to my level, turns to face me, then slowly lifts her black-tinted goggles up and away from her eyes and I watch intently. I fear my mouth is agape as she reveals the most mesmerising pair of azure-blue eyes I – or, I would suggest, the world – has ever seen. The effect causes me to fall backwards and I slump down pathetically into the water, speechless. All I can do is stare, transfixed, into precipitous shades of blue.

'Well, I'm just starting back again after a few years off from swimming,' she replies, with complete innocence. 'I hope to make it here a couple of times a week to start with.'

I'm staring, and I know I'm staring quite obviously, but it is hard to stop. I could well be dribbling, too. I'm conscious it is probably my turn to say something, so I fumble, 'Great. Marvellous,' while nodding my head vigorously. There's another momentary pause while I try to get my act together.

'Welcome back, then. The water's missed you!' I laugh nervously and fortunately she's kind enough to do the same.

'You, er, staying on for a coffee?'

'Yes, I thought I would,' she replies with a broad smile. 'I'll see you upstairs in the bar, then.'

'Er, good. Yes, okay. Oh, I'm Seacombe, by the way. That's my name.'

'Hello. Yes. I know. I heard. I'm Katherine, and I'm new,' she adds teasingly.

She slips her hand beneath her swim cap and allows a bundle of dark brown hair streaked with shades of light auburn to unfurl and fall onto her shoulders. She shakes it out and runs her fingers casually through a few twisted curls. It's like a waterfall released from the confines of a dam. Her actions have me mesmerised pathetically once more. Chestnut hair and electric blue eyes, an unearthly and striking combination. I am astonished. My God!

'See you up there in a minute.' And she bounces up onto the poolside.

I slope back into the pool and, like a seal that's momentarily popped its head up for a look-see, slowly sink beneath the water, disappearing from view. I push off underwater and swim a length with one breath, a grin the width of the Grand Canyon stretched across my face.

10:30

Coffee time.

One of the joys of this particular swimming pool is the way in which the coffee bar overlooks the pool so you can watch the swimmers from above while chatting with friends. This morning it's busy, with most of the tables already taken, so I wander over to the long glass window and join the already flowing conversation. I keep an eye out for Katherine, but she hasn't made it up from the changing rooms yet.

A little while later I hear a soft voice behind me and turn around eagerly. For a moment, I allow myself to take in what's in front of me. I am briefly thrown because she is, umm, well, er… clothed. Her face is no longer framed by a black swim hat and her hair, still slightly damp and tangled, hangs loosely. She's a foot shorter than me and so I look down into those alluring, hypnotising eyes. Her smile is vast and it's difficult not to reciprocate. She stands with her feet slightly outwards – like a ballet dancer – with one hand casually placed on her hip while she gesticulates with the other.

'Hello,' I say. 'You—'

'Hiya, Katherine, good swim?' Friend John butts in.

'Well, it's all a bit of a shock to the system right now. I've been too long away from the water, and it feels like a lot of hard work,' she replies modestly.

'Could have fooled me! Wish I could move through the water like you do,' he says, looking over at me for confirmation. 'So, where have you been for the past few years?' he continues.

'Having children. Doing the family thing!' She laughs. 'I have three now. Two boys and a girl. The boys are doing trampolining this morning while I swim, and Anna's at a new dance class.'

I catch John's eye and know he's thinking the same thing as me. This woman just doesn't look old enough to have three kids.

'So, how old are they?' he enquires.

'Anna is six, Michael is eight and Robert, the oldest, is ten,' she says proudly.

'Bet they keep you busy. I've got three lads and they wear me out.'

'I seem to be very fortunate, all three are very good really, well… for the moment,' she says, then chuckles to herself.

I am in no rush to leave and prepare to dig in for a caffeine overload in the hope the others, but not Katherine, will have to disappear soon.

Sure enough, two coffees later and we're standing by ourselves. I ask Katherine if she has to shoot off anywhere and she shakes her head.

'I'm okay for a little while,' she says, looking at the wall clock, so we grab an empty table and pull up a couple of chairs.

'I can see that you enjoy the water,' she says.

'In it. On it. By it. That's my simple philosophy for life,' I state. 'Although I do like the hills and mountains as well.'

My response has her attention and she's looking at me intently. I continue, 'After swimming, my next love is kayaking.' She leans further forward towards me sliding her elbows across the table. I sense her heightened interest.

'Kayaking. On the sea?'

'Yes, most of the time. If the weather's a bit crap I'll go on the rivers, but generally it's out on the sea and along the coastline, or in and around Poole Harbour. There's always so much to discover and I adore the freedom, it's the big escape.'

Her questions begin to flow and become more specific. I answer each carefully in some length and in detail – possibly too much detail – and soon realise I sound very much like a nerd, so I stop. But she is absorbing everything I say. It turns out Katherine did a bit of kayaking in her teens, but since living in Dorset has not had the opportunity to get back out on the water. I find myself saying, 'You should give it another go.' Without thinking of the consequences, I add, 'Why don't you come out paddling with me sometime? I've got a spare boat.'

A silence.

Then.

'I'd absolutely love to. When?'

She has caught me off balance and I can't think straight. I answer randomly, 'What about next Friday afternoon?'

'Perfect. Fridays are always good for me.'

'Great. Fab,' I splutter. 'Er, next week it is then!'

JUNE

'You have opened my eyes and
I fear there may be no going back '

Tuesday 1st June

14:00

I'm at a suppliers meeting with Graham, bored and doodling in my notebook. '*I Am A Sea Of Intrigue. Discuss.*'

I look across to see Graham still deep in conversation with our merchants, so begin to set down my thoughts:

- ***Who is she?*** *(bold and underlined a dozen times)*
- *Where has she come from? (outer space?)*
- *But, why land here in Dorset?*
- *And why now?*
- *And with whom?*
- *Are the kids aliens too?*
- *What's it like on her planet?*
- *She loves the water, perhaps hers is an inundated planet? Or perhaps there is water no more like in* The Man Who Fell To Earth*?*
- *Perhaps she really lives under the water. An amphibious subterranean being?*
- *Maybe she's been ordered here, on a secret mission to seek me out… and to help, er… continue her species?*

I notice Graham's looking over to me. 'Are you with us, Seacombe?'

'Yes, yes, I'm all ears,' I say, and shuffle forwards to re-join the conversation.

Wednesday 2nd June

10:00
Bright F2-3, SW, +19°
Training: ↑
Work forecast: ↑

Just back off the water. Lovely early morning paddle around the harbour islands and back up towards Wareham. No one else out so had the water to myself; just me and the birdlife in the harbour. Perfect. And now I'm motivated to get on with some work; a proactive day sat in front of my computer writing emails and putting in the business calls. Yeah!

11:15
A text from Lois:

<Sorrrry to disturb. Can you call? Big favour needed X>

<Oks, will do>

Bugger! Lois needs a lift to the airport. Her normally reliable VW has expired through lack of oil. I told her to keep checking it! And her flight is tonight – midnight tonight, a confusing early Thursday morning departure. So have said I'll head over soon and be there by teatime.

18:30
I arrive to find that Lois has still barely packed her bags and there are clothes scattered over the hallway, bathroom and bedroom floor while

she's still hunting for her passport, last seen supposedly in the top drawer by the right-hand side of the bed. Marvellous!

'You're a nightmare,' I shout loudly.

'Yesss, I'm sorry. I was so organised and then I couldn't find my passport. It's here somewhere.'

'Okay. When was the last time you had it in your hand?'

'Umm, when I booked the tickets, I think.'

'Have you got your tickets?'

'Umm. They must be with the passport.'

'Oh, great.'

We search the house high and low and Lois checks through her coat pockets. I head for the spare bedroom-cum-office and attempt to get to the computer – if I can find the computer under the piles of paperwork and unsorted paraphernalia. It has to be in here somewhere, surely this is the most obvious place. I sit at the desk and glance around the room. Ah-ha. What's that white pocket folder doing by the pot plants?

'Found it,' I shout. 'Behind your bloody pansies!'

Lois walks in. 'Sorry, must have put it there when I was watering the plants.'

23:30

Have dropped Miss Scatterbrain off at the airport and now a long drive back to base. At least at this time of night there shouldn't be any traffic. With luck will be home and out cold by 2am. I need the sleep.

Thursday 3rd June

11:00
*Summer's here F2-3, SW, +23°
Training: ↑
Work forecast: ←→

Text from Lois.

> *<Thank u, thank u, many hugs arrived ok. Beach is lovely and u'd look good on it! Missing you already XXX>*

> *<Yor supposed to be working?! Get to it. Lots x>*

12:00
Swim training tonight and I have made a particular effort not to think about the fact that Katherine may well be there.

18:50
At the pool.

Oh crikey, there she is – already in the water! Am I late? No. I can't be. Wow, she must be keen.

I jump into the empty lane with a manly splash and then leap to the surface, trying to impress but probably failing. She looks at me as if I'm a little mad as I greet her with, 'Evening. What a lovely day it's been, hasn't it?' She beams her beam and nods enthusiastically in agreement.

'Okay for paddling tomorrow?' I ask quickly.

'Yes,' she replies. Then lowers her voice as if she's about to tell me a secret. 'I've managed to get about three hours free. Is that going to be enough?'

'How far were you planning to go! That should be ample. Meet at Lake Pier, Hamworthy. I'll have everything you need. 1.30pm. Okay?'

'Great. See you tomorrow afternoon then.'

21:45

What an exhilarating swim session it was. I was flying. Felt really relaxed in the water; everything seemed so easy tonight. Wasn't far off my PB for a 400m either. Katherine was motoring too and there is no way I can get near her on backstroke or butterfly. She led the lane on both those strokes.

Friday 4th June

13:30

*Summer's def here F2-3, SW, +25°

'A man who is not afraid of the sea
will soon be drowned, he said
for he will be going out on a day he shouldn't'
(John Millington Synge 1871–1909)

The very moment she climbed out of her rather scruffy black Saab… I knew I was in trouble.

I am transfixed by her cream classic-cut linen dress that emphasises the shape of her shoulders and accentuates her naked, tanned arms. Her palms open outwards to greet me. The veins running down the inside length of her forearms are pronounced and curiously attractive. She's moving towards me too quickly and I struggle to soak up everything that I hunger to see. She's fit, shapely and the way she walks is overwhelmingly sexy.

I sit underneath the tailgate of the car watching and am tempted to greet her with a kiss on the cheek but resist the urge.

'Nice to see you,' I say, somewhat shakily. 'It's going to be a fabulous day for a paddle.'

'Oh, yes, I've been looking forward to this.'

So have I, I say to myself. If only she had an inkling of the number of idle hours I've spent thinking about this moment. How I would first greet her when she arrived and how together I would appear. Rather than the bundle of adolescent nerves, the adrenalin-soaked idiot that's floundering in front of her now.

I turn to the two kayaks on the roof of my car and begin to prattle on about each boat: the different types of construction, different hull designs, cockpit types, rudder styles, the importance of boat trim and so on, endlessly. All the time, she's standing there quietly taking it in – well, appears to be taking it all in. My monologue lasts for a good ten minutes before I realise I'm making a *boring ass of myself.*

'Is this one mine?' she asks, and points towards my boat, my really-quite-expensive new, bright tangerine-coloured lightweight carbon kayak.

'Well, it could be, but you'd probably be better off in this one.' I point to my smaller orange and black, and slightly more play-worn, kayak.

'It's about smiles-per-mile and in that kayak I think you might struggle after the first few minutes. It's a bit tippy. However, this orange-and-black chap is actually my first ever kayak and gives guaranteed multiple grins. I'm very fond of him. We've some good memories. He's stable, solid and very predictable; I think you'll like the ride.'

'Oh, I'm sure I will,' Katherine says excitedly. 'But aren't all boats supposed to be called "she"?'

'Of course, but I prefer to call it a "he". He's been a good mate and got me out of all sorts of watery troubles, particularly on rough and windy days when I probably shouldn't have been out! He has never let me down.'

'Well, I'm looking forward to being with him,' she says with a smirk across her face.

Katherine nips off to change into her sea-going gear (Lycra tights and Lycra top), and together we carry the kayaks down to the beach and place them together on the sand. Sea conditions are perfect today; the sky is an implausible blue and there's a light warm breeze blowing down from the west, creating nothing more than a few ripples on the surface of the water. Despite the high tide, only small waves casually lap the shore. Gulls glide effortlessly overhead, and oystercatchers garrulously make themselves heard while the few bathers on the beach enjoy the early June sunshine.

Katherine moves down to the shoreline, scoops up two handfuls of water and throws them onto her face, then buries her head into her wet palms and rubs them all over her cheeks and hair.

I say nothing but note the moment.

I suggest she try the boat for size while it is on the beach. She sits in easily and I kneel down beside her on the sand. I detect new scents: part salt, part fragrant shampoo, part skin, part her. She wiggles in the seat, then reaches forward to the footplate bending past my face.

'It fits like a glove!' she says excitedly.

'Seems to.'

I'm feeling calmer now. The rush of adrenalin has diluted; I am not sorry it's gone and am content to stay kneeling, supplicant-like, at Katherine's side.

'We should probably check you can get your spray deck off just in case you capsize.' I straddle the front deck of the boat and face towards her, my legs splayed either side of the hull. I demonstrate what needs to be done a number of times with the spray deck and I see Katherine's face looking a little flushed.

We get the boats onto the water and begin to head over to Arne slowly; I shout a few words of advice but there's not much I need to teach this girl. She's at one with the boat straight away.

We cruise to the islands and I pull closer alongside so we can chat more easily. The place is deserted except for the wildlife that scuttles busily by the shore and over the tall reed beds. The breeze gets up, creating larger wavelets that slap gently against the hulls and the resulting soporific sound resonates throughout the boats. Katherine is looking around in wonderment, then glances over to me and I immediately feel great contentment. I realise I've not felt this calm inside with anyone before.

We paddle between the islands and our conversation begins to find its own rhythm. Firstly, about where we are and the simple joy of our movement and the landscape we're in, but soon we move on to our lives.

I supply her with my story. She seems interested in what I have to say and then asks, 'So, do you live alone, or do you have a girlfriend?'

Caught unawares, I reply, 'Yes. Yes, I have had a girlfriend for a few years now. Her name is Lois.'

'That's an unusual name. Do you live together?'

'No. I see her most weekends and occasionally during the week. She lives a bit of a way away from me, you understand?'

'Oh, I see.'

A few paddle strokes later.

'I can't believe you have three children. You look too, well, young!'

'Ha-ha. You're kind. I'm much older than you probably imagine.'

'Well, you certainly look well cared for and with very low mileage. Are you, er, in fact, er, married?'

'Yes, I am – for thirteen years now.'

'Really… wow!'

I paddle on ahead metaphorically shaking my head. *Wow, thirteen years*, I say to myself, *lucky man, wow.*

As we approach the sandy shores of Gold Point, I suggest we pull the boats up on the beach and take a five-minute break. Katherine's happy with the idea. We slide the kayaks up onto the sand and perch ourselves on the front decks. We look down the length of the harbour as the warm sea breeze gently blows against our faces. The waves are lapping around our feet and we study how they sink deeper into the sand as the waves wash over them. Katherine is talking but I am not hearing what she is saying. I turn my head to the left to look at her and all I see are her lips moving up and down as if in slow motion. I cannot hear a sound. I'm spellbound by the movement, the ripeness they possess, and the delicate changing curves of each one as they come together then move apart in perfect choreography. There is certainly sound being moderated by such beautiful motion, but my senses are in overload and nothing is registering. She smiles, but still I look on captivated by the shape of her mouth. She looks at me inquisitively, says something, but still I don't hear it. She repeats herself. This time it brings me back from my hypnotised state.

'Sorry. What?'

'I was saying how lucky you are to be able to enjoy all this. This adventure land.'

'Ah, yes. I never take it for granted. It is the life I've chosen.'

We put the boats back in and head off up the harbour. The tide is starting to turn and the water is gaining more movement. We cross the main channel at its narrowest point and make our way back closer to the shore. Katherine says she's thirsty and asks to take a sip of water from my drinks bottle. I manoeuvre my boat around and come alongside her to make it easier to pass the container across. The kayaks are facing in opposite directions and she's right next to my shoulder and for the very first time, we are close to one another. I put my hand in my lifejacket pocket and pull out the water bottle while holding onto her kayak with my other hand. Katherine leans over towards me a fraction as I pass the water over and, inadvertently, our fingers entwine around the bottle and – *baaaam*! – there's a lightning strike! A *huge* powerful electric jolt has us both instantly recoiling. The bottle falls between the boats and we look at one another in total and utter bewilderment, stunned by what has just happened.

Katherine's eyes are wide open, her mouth agape. My head is spinning wildly, and I'm totally confounded. I look at Katherine with a deeply puzzled expression. The electric shock wasn't particularly painful in any way; it just had an intense power to throw us backwards. What on earth just happened? The touching of our fingers for the very first time creating a massive spark of electrical energy.

The boats are drifting apart and begin to pirouette this way and that in the flow of the current, but we sit motionless and silent, trying to figure out what had just taken place between us.

After a short while and very slowly, we paddle back to the launch spot, gathering ourselves together without a word being spoken.

Ashore, I begin to clean the boats down, still in a confused state, as Katherine changes into her dry clothes. She then walks around to my car and leans casually against the side as I sit tidying various pieces of kit away.

'Thank you for today,' she says softly. 'A few *surprises* indeed… ha-ha… and you were right – a good many smiles too.'

I look up at her. 'My pleasure. My pleasure for sure. You will come again?'

She pauses for a moment, then, with a somewhat cheeky grin says, 'Yes. Yes, this is something I'd *really* like to do again.'

TWO DAYS LATER

Monday 7th June

08:50
*Summer's on, +26°
Grin size: XL
CD player volume: High

Am concerned Springsteen's album 'The Rising' is going to get worn away to oblivion. The CD is definitely getting thinner.

Bloody great album, shame no one else appreciates my singing though. Katherine might just. No! Don't mention the K word, you fool! No, no, no, no, no. I've been trying to cage her up, put her under lock and key and double-bolt the door, but still she escapes. How *does she do it*? Like Houdini, she defies the odds and wriggles free of all the chains I've been placing meticulously around her and then pulling overly tight.

11:55
She's been on my mind all morning. In the nicest possible way of course, so I can't complain, but still I am fascinated by who she is. The urge to discover more is undeniable. And what was that powerful electric shock/spark/bolt of lightning thing all about? Repressed energy finally being allowed to be released? Never heard of that happening before between two people. Quite surreal. An incredibly special feeling, that's for sure.

But she *is* married with *three* young children, has a seemingly perfect life; why would I want to create any form of upset? And I have a girlfriend. A very lovely girlfriend who does love me.

13:40
Perhaps she is like this with everyone? I know she is naturally friendly,

so maybe I'm the crazy one here with all the questions and she is just naturally like this with all her male friends. It's just me getting completely messed up. I think it has to be me.

It has to be one sided. But… could she be feeling the same though? Just even an itsy-bitsy little bit?

No. Don't be so stupid.

14:50

Just a thought. Why isn't she wearing a wedding ring?

Maybe she is and I just didn't notice?

Wednesday 9th June

11:50
*Flaming June +25°
Training: ↑
Work forecast: ↑

Is it Thursday yet?

Thursday 10th June

07:15
*Hot still +26°
Training: ↑
Work forecast: ↑

13:45
Lunchtime. And the K word has only crept once into my busy morning – just a teeny fraction. I've been very good; the chains have been holding up nicely and there's only a few hours – well, an afternoon – to get through before they may be… unleashed, and I'm able to think about her legally. Er, is that the right expression?

19:00
Swim time.

Hah! There she is. Oh no, she's standing in lane 2. Not in lane 1. What's going on?

Swim coach Mark shouts, 'Let's get going now, less of the chatter. We're doing something slightly different tonight. Jean, you lead lane 3, Katherine, lane 2 and Seacombe, lane 1. It's all medley work.'

Oh crap! Individual medley. Not my forte at all. I grovel on butterfly, fall asleep on backstroke, wake up a bit on breaststroke, then just about get going on front crawl. Why doesn't someone else take the lead in my lane? Or better still, let Katherine lead me, she's a proper medley swimmer.

It's a busy session tonight with five or six people per lane, and everyone seems to be buzzing on something. Must be the hot weather that has got into everyone, me included. I've yet to catch K's attention and I'm desperate. Each time I look across, someone is either standing in front of her blocking my view or chatting away to her. Annoying.

The session starts and it is eyeballs out for the first short set – but I plan it so that as the distances get longer and more turns become involved, I might be able to time it to tumble turn at the exact same moment as K and grab her attention under water.

The set changes and, with luck, my scheme has a chance of working. K sets off in lane 2 and I deliberately head off slowly and, with clear water in front of me, can see K's little feet kicking away like a metronome to one side of me. As the turn comes up, I accelerate towards the wall, tumble quickly, and then push off as hard as I can and glide under water. I grab a perfect, undisturbed view of K, who's executing the same manoeuvre. She sees what I am doing and smiles broadly just before she surfaces. Another lap and we do it again; this time we both come off the wall at exactly the same moment and push off in unison, looking at one another and grinning like mischievous schoolchildren. Another lap, and we do it again, and then again, and again, each one timed perfectly and rewarded equally.

Oh, what a good game!

As that set ends, I start to get the giggles – partly because it's so silly and juvenile and er, partly because it's all so silly and juvenile. I catch K's eye – and she's giggling too.

The session continues. Mark throws in some killer sprint sets, which has us all gasping for air and absolutely no time for any further underwater synchro, but as the whistle blows, magically I'm alongside K and am determined to speak with her.

'Recovered all right from the paddling?' I say, panting.

'Ah, yes I have, thank you,' she replies. 'I really enjoyed my time on the water, it was lovely.'

She pauses. Clearly there's something on her mind.

Coyly she adds, 'Do you think… mmm… would you… er—'

'Yes?'

'C-could we go out in the kayaks again sometime soon?'

Inwardly, I am glowing. 'For sure. Of course. Let me check my diary and get back to you.'

'Great!' she says, seeing through my bullshit. 'You do that then please, Mister.'

We walk slowly to the changing rooms and I'm in no rush to see her disappear behind the screens. All I want to do is absorb more of her while she's standing next to me. Adore this vision-in-black. She has been gifted a physique – in my eyes – of almost perfect body symmetry. A firm hour-glass shape with swimmer's shoulders and a strong athletic torso. How she has kept herself in such amazing shape having brought three children into this world defies me.

The truth is, she must get many admiring glances wherever she goes, but somehow I get the distinct impression any such attention simply passes her by.

Friday 11th June

09:15
Not the best sleep I have ever had, I admit; fitful. I was up pacing about the house at 2am and again at 4am. She won't get out of my head.

10:30
Kettle's on. Must get on with some work. Must, must, must. Graham's on my case and there are things to be done. Money to be earnt.

10:40
Phone is buzzing. A text message. Unknown number.

<Hello. Katherine here. Forgot to give you my mobile number. Katherine>

Eh? What? Crikey, she's keen! How did she get my number? I wonder where she got it from. Anyway, doesn't matter. Now I've got hers!

Better send an acknowledgement.

<Seacombe receiving here! Thank you.>

10:42
Hah! All of a sudden, I feel totally becalmed. Oh, I wonder why that is! Such is the powerful effect this woman is having on me.

10:45
Anyway, to all things work. Lots to do.

21:30

Racing tomorrow. 10km kayak time trial on the River Avon. Nothing too serious but it has the word 'race' in it, so best get early night's sleep. Let's hope I can.

But, somehow, I think sleep will come easier now.

Monday 14th June

09:05
*Hot still +28!

Text message – and it's from K!

<Did I say thank you for the other day out in the harbour? Would like to say more but not easy on this. Katherine>

Crikey! What do I do now? Respond immediately? Respond later? Not respond at all? No, not that one, can't do that!

A few minutes later and there's another!

<Are you swimming this Thursday? Katherine>

09:10
What shall I do? Play it cool, be ever so nonchalant.

She clearly wants to speak with me. Or something. Oh no!

I'm sensing I could get myself into a whole world of trouble here if I'm not very careful.

09:22

<Yes! See you in the water 7pm>

Gives me a couple of days to sort my head out.

Argh!

10:45

I'm waiting for Graham at our usual service station rendezvous. We're off to meet a new client. He's late as usual but no problem, it gives me an opportunity to draw up some very important lists:

Top 10 favourite bits:

1. *her blue eyes*
2. *her big smile*
3. *her sexy mouth*
4. *her soothing, oh-so lovely voice*
5. *her hips*
6. *her size*
7. *her flat tummy*
8. *her arms*
9. *her smell*
10. *her hair*

Top 10 favourite bits: in alphabetical order:

1. *arms*
2. *eyes*
3. *hair*
4. *hips*
5. *mouth*
6. *size*
7. *smell*
8. *smile*
9. *tummy*
10. *voice*

Top 10 favourite bits if I was wearing a blindfold (but could touch):

1. *her hips*
2. *her soothing, oh-so lovely voice*
3. *her laugh*
4. *her breath*

5. *her smell*
6. *her hair*
7. *her flat tummy*
8. *her arms*
9. *her sexy mouth*
10. *her overwhelming aura of peacefulness*

Top 10 least favourite bits (actually, only 2):

1. *Married*
2. *Girlfriend*

14:40
Back home and the work meeting went quite well and there indeed might be some 'traction' – as they like to say in this world – with the potential client. I've more product detail to fax over to them and that's something I can prepare with Graham's help later in the week.

16:00
Something strange has been on my mind this afternoon and I just can't work it out. It's the fact that, quite conversely, of course, I would love to hold K in my arms but at the same time it's almost as if *I don't need to*. Being with her on the water, standing close to her, swimming with her feels almost as if *that's enough*. Simply being in her company is nourishment indeed.

16:05
...or enough for now?

18:30
Am very tempted to text K. But I give in to Lois and send her a message instead.

18:31

> *<Have found us some possible holiday destinations. How u getting on with the job out there X?>*

Thursday 17th June

19:00
Training: ↑
Work forecast: ↑

Swim training.

I've been ridiculously chirpy all day, nice to everyone, laughed, smiled, felt sorry for people – all sorts of peculiarities – and importantly, highly proactive on the work front. All because I'm due to see K at any minute. She said she was going to be here.

'Right, lane 1 and 2, get your warm-up underway,' shouts Mark.

Still no sign of her.

19:10

'Okay. Lane 1, this is your main set,' (points to the board). 'Lane 2, this is yours. Let's get going.'

Oh no! Where is she? If she's not here by now, then clearly, she's not coming. Was it something I said? Or didn't say?

19:30

I'm leading the lane, but I feel really down. I can't believe the way I'm reacting to all this. I hardly know her and yet I'm already depressed she's not here and weirdly concerned for her. How bloody crazy is this? It can't be normal. Maybe I need to see someone. Someone who wears a white jacket.

21:35

Back home and drinking tea.

<Did you swim? Had ill child who needed my attention at v last minute. Will be there Sat. Fingers xrossed. Katherine>

<OK, Flipper. See you in the water>

Thank heavens! She's fine. Phew! I can relax. My world is now sorted!

I must remind her that she doesn't need to write her name after every text message.

Though, I do find it quite endearing.

TWO DAYS LATER

Monday 21st June

10:00
Training: ↑
Work forecast: ↑

Been thinking about something all weekend and I know it is *not* a sensible idea! Could lead to all sorts of issues, but… I just don't know.

It's a date that gets scribbled in my diary every year in the hope that I can get to go – the Henley Royal Regatta, a11 week on the Thames. It's finals day next weekend. Thing is, should I ask K to come *with me* – in the kayaks?

I weigh up the pluses and minuses and churn them over in my mind. Aside from the upset if Lois were to find out, what's the problem?

10:45
Balls to it. Succumbed. What real harm can it do? She can only say no!

> *<Henley Regatta next Saturday up on the Thames. Forget swim training. Fancy watching the rowing from a nice orange kayak?>*

10:50

> *<Yes. Sounds wonderful. Would love to very much. But must be home by 7pm. Is that OK? Katherine>*

Result!

FIVE DAYS LATER

Saturday 26th June

06:00
Good but a few scruffy clouds about

'Let your boat of life be light, packed with only what you need.'
(J. K. Jerome 1859–1927)

It's felt like a very long week. The moment K accepted my invite, I've wished every day would get out of the bleedin' way. Not seen her since Monday and have had a heavy week travelling on business stuff, which has been good, but I missed swim training on Thursday as I was just too knackered.

06:15
It's only a short drive down to the swimming pool, where I said I'd meet Katherine, and from there it's a couple of hours or so beyond the borders of Dorset to the River Thames and on to Henley.

I pull into the empty car park, park up and wait for a few moments. Prince is playing on the radio.

'The most beautiful girl in the world'

A black car pulls in next to me.

'Morning,' I say, in my fake West Country accent.

'Hey, you,' K says chirpily as she bounds from her car, then hops lightly from one foot to the other as if she's either quite cold, needs the loo or is actually quite excited. I presume the latter and don't make an issue about the other two.

'You gotta be back here by 7pm, right?' I check.

'Yes, please, I have to be. Children!'

'Okay then, let's be on our way and get on *that river*!'

Two and a half hours later, after some light and enjoyable conversation in the car, we're unloading the two orange boats from the roof and onto the bank of the Thames.

The Regatta has not changed over the years, and that is what makes it so much fun to attend. I've worked out that I have been going to this event, on and off, for more than twenty-eight years, since my school days. My mother would often take us along by rowing boat after school had finished. We'd tie up by the finish line to watch the racing. Over the years since, I seem to have found a way of making it to the Regatta one way or another, and it's never lost its appeal.

There's something very English and traditional about it that has defied the ravages of time, avoiding the absurd amount of commercialism that has overtaken most other sporting events.

Along with Wimbledon, Goodwood, and possibly Ascot, there are not many events that have that depth of sporting history and retain an appropriate period look. Henley is a gathering for those who have an affinity with *liquid history* and the River Thames in particular. It's such a wonderful stretch of water.

Our launching point is a couple of miles downstream of the Regatta course at Aston, which means a short paddle to the start line, and then along the Regatta course itself to the finish line some two miles further on.

We launch the boats and amazingly we're the only people about in this little river space. We soak up the atmosphere – the unique, characterful smell of the Thames, which is so different from any other water I know. While lakes and other freshwater streams can have a similar odour – and the sea, of course, has its own magical fragrance – the Thames has a pungency that is distinctly *the* Thames. There is simply no hiding from it: unpleasant, though, it is not.

K settles into her boat and we head down the mirror-smooth

water towards a little back creek I want to show her. The sun is warm when it is allowed out from behind the clouds and the reflection off the water and the deck of the kayak causes momentary blindness. I stop to put on my sunglasses. As I fumble for the case in my pocket, I hear a familiar sound and immediately alert K. 'Look, there… a kingfisher.' The iridescent streak flies from the riverbank, low across the front of the boats, calling, as the sun catches its blue-green-turquoise colours.

K is ecstatic. 'Wow! That's my favourite bird and the first time I've seen one close up. Gosh! That's made my day already.'

We paddle through the quiet back creek, then re-join the river and head up towards the Regatta course, aware that the present tranquillity will soon be left behind.

We approach the spectator side of the river some way past the start point; the clouds are beginning to gather and it looks like there might be a downpour. A classic summer shower! Sure enough, a few minutes later, the rain moves rapidly up the course towards us, blown by a gusting wind. It has people running for cover. Brightly coloured umbrellas appear in the grandstands like rapidly blooming flowers. The men in the crowd are hurriedly covering their heads with their striped rowing jackets. Women in long dresses, summer hats and heels squeal as they run for shelter. We quickly steer the boats towards the riverbank and manage to find an overhanging willow that offers some protection. I pull K's boat next to mine and hang onto the bank with one hand, and we sit crouched in the boats listening to the fat raindrops fall loudly.

Then, something extraordinary happens between us.

The wind is gusting hard and to hold on to K's boat securely, I have to put my hand inside the cockpit and, without intending it, my fingers touch her thigh. *Baaaam*! I receive a huge electric jolt – *again*! My arm recoils immediately at the force of the shock. I'm stunned at the strength and I see K looking at me with eyes wide like saucers; her expression is an equal mix of surprise and wonderment.

Cautiously, I place my hand back again inside the cockpit, this time carefully making sure to avoid her thigh. We sit motionless in our boats, not saying anything. We try to make some sense of what has just happened – for the second time!

The shower moves off and we emerge from beneath the branches to paddle down towards the finish line in the hope of finding a space on the booms. I know we can moor up there and watch the rowers power their way past us to the finish flag at full speed. K is enthralled by the sight of the Women's Four racing.

'I would like to have a go at that. Do you think I'd be able to do it?' she asks.

'I'm certain you could. You'd be very good at it too, especially with your level of fitness.'

I can see her mind churning over the idea, and so we wait for the next race, the Women's Eight. As the crews thunder past, no more than a metre and a half away from our kayaks, the sense of raw power and intensity of effort is overwhelming. You can feel the physical effort involved as each crew member gives their all in the last-gasp attempt to race their boats to the flag. Emotions are high, none more so than when the second-place crews drop their heads as they cross the line. All that training, dedication and lifestyle commitment, only to end up defeated.

As that was the last race before the hour-long lunch break, I suggest we go in search of replenishment. We paddle down towards Marsh Lock to a café I know that will serve itinerant river strays by the water's edge.

We sit on the grass, our boats by our side.

'So, what do you want out of life?' I ask, trying to learn more about this intriguing woman.

'Well… I want to enjoy watching my children grow up, of course, and I wouldn't mind living for a very long time, just like my grandma. She lived to be 103, you know… She was so fit and young at heart and so sharp right to the end, amazing really. There's so much going on around us and I want to experience just as much as possible – live life – as they say. Just as long as I'm fit and healthy to appreciate it.'

'Yeah, too right,' I reply. 'I don't really do ill.'

'Nor me. I'm never ill.'

'If you can't participate because you're out of shape or stuck indoors all day, it's not a real life. It's not much fun being one of life's constant spectators.'

'But, isn't that what we are doing today? Being spectators?'

'Hah, I suppose so, and we are sitting on our backsides, so yes, we are officially spectators.'

'What about you?' she asks. 'What do you want out of life?'

'How long have you got? Well, I suppose my ambitions have changed as I've grown older and now, I want a simpler life. One perhaps less grand and with less risk, limited hassle, and minimal stress, and of course a life with someone who is firmly on my wavelength and who enjoys the same simple pleasures – all the natural things around us, I suppose.'

'But don't you have that already?'

'Yes, I guess I do, it's just not, well, not quite how I envisaged it. It is good though, so don't get me wrong.'

'What do you *envisage*?'

I'm stumped by K's question. I know what I'd really like to say is, *with someone who makes me feel as enriched and as comforted and as warm inside as you do*. But I wimp out.

'Don't you think we should be doing more of that spectating stuff again? Racing will begin again shortly.'

'Okay then, yes, let's go and watch more of the rowing!' K says. She's looking at me as if to say, *You coward*!

We lift the boats back onto the river and set off downstream at a steady pace.

I just can't help noticing how at ease she is with the water. Paddling, she's very relaxed in the boat, with a strong paddle stroke and a good sense of stability. I know from training with her in the pool and watching her move through the water that she is at one and calm with her surroundings. Her natural speed, grace, elegance and efficiency is a delight to the eye. I'm certain she must have been a water baby – introduced at a very early age – and has fallen in sync with the liquid.

Not wanting to head back downriver, because that means heading home, we amble back alongside the Regatta course, soaking up more of the atmosphere. Wherever we look, wherever we go, people are having a wonderful time. Other boaters make favourable comments about our kayaks, joking and chatting with us, making us feel very much part of everything.

I look back over my left shoulder to check on K and she gives me a smile as big and beamy as Jack Nicholson's Joker. It has me wobbling in my boat. Her contented smile says it all. No need for words. This is it. The way she looks directly at me is the wax seal placed firmly on the bottom of a very important, long-term, unbreakable contract. Oh yes, sir!

17:20

We're driving back down the motorway towards Dorset and K is happy to talk about her home life.

'Tim doesn't like the water. He's not a fan. Never has been. In fact, he cannot understand my need to swim. To him it's all pointless. Actually, he thinks all of us at the swimming club are mentally ill!'

'What?'

'Seriously. He thinks we all have something missing.'

'Well, that's charming.'

'He doesn't like wasted energy. He's a perfectionist at everything he does – likes things to be exact and just so. He enjoys his music, photography and his cars, which he's always fiddling about with in his spare time. Our driveway is a car lot but he's very good at it. He seems to have a sixth sense when it comes to mechanical things.'

'Ah, come to think of it, I think I've seen him outside at the pool a couple of times recently, sitting in a green VW camper, presumably waiting for you. Longish blond hair, goatee beard, fair skinned, very slim, very good looking?'

'Yes, that's him – and that's the camping bus, a recent purchase. The children adore it and we've had some great camping trips in it already, but it's been a mechanical horror story. Not been a good buy!'

'What's he do for a job, if you don't mind me asking?'

'Medicine. He's a GP, but he spent several years working for Médecins Sans Frontières. When we first got together – I was the young nurse and he was the good-looking doctor. How's that for a cliché? I hardly ever saw him. He was in charge of field hospitals during several international conflicts. I think it has affected his outlook. These days his practice is at a surgery close to the house.'

'Aha! That's why you're never ill, then. You have your own personal physician.'

'Ha-ha. Yes. Perhaps there's a bit of that in our relationship. He's very attentive—'

'I don't know how you do it. How you manage to organise your busy life and your family.'

'Well, they all help out, so I can't complain. Everything is really local to us. Daily life is actually pretty sorted.'

'Why don't you wear a wedding ring, then?'

'I do, actually, but not when swimming as it keeps falling off and gets in the way, so I take it off quite a lot.'

We gradually fall silent and for the rest of the journey the radio remains switched off – no music, no noise, just the slight melodic whistle of the wind through the boat roof rack. It's a comfortable silence. Joyously so. There's no urgent need to say anything, just a feeling of quiet companionship. K is looking out the side window with a dreamy look, and I'm happy to focus on the driving while I hear my inner voice endlessly repeating, *This-woman-is-contented-in-my-*

company-and-I-am-contented-in-hers,this-woman-is-contented-in-my-company-and-I-am-contented-in-hers.

We arrive at the pool car park with twelve minutes to spare. K hops out, picks up her kit bag from the backseat and then puts it in her boot. We then stand opposite one another. Neither of us knows what to do next. Should I go in for the hug and kiss her on the cheek (could be dangerous), or should I shake her hand and say something like 'thank you for today and I hope to see you again soon' (er, no), or spin round and hop back in to my seat and wave a jolly goodbye? (a definite no).

For a few painful, awkward seconds, we stand apart like gunfighters at the OK Corral, waiting for someone to make the next move.

I go for a wry smile, like Clint Eastwood's, only cooler, while K pushes her tongue to the side of her mouth, then bites her lip. I kick the car tyre with my flip-flop, then wish I hadn't. K puts her hands in her pockets, then pulls them back out again. I chuckle nervously, but we're at an impasse. Nobody is going anywhere.

More seconds of discomfiture, then K draws with the speed that would have defeated both Wyatt and Virgil Earp. She fires a single shot and scores a direct hit to the heart.

'You know,' she says, 'you have opened my eyes and I fear there may be no going back—'

I'm thrown backwards and slump onto my car seat and euphorically… feel my heart ooze the colour gold.

Oh, flippin' heck!

What the bloody hell do I do now?

Monday 28th June

07:30
Brightening up, +19°
Grin size: XL
Office forecast: ↑
Exercise outlook: ↑

Text from K!

> *<Did I leave some clothing in your car? Sorry!>*

I go to check the boot of my car and take a rummage round. Sure enough, tucked up behind the front passenger seat is a semi-damp swim towel and inside – her paddling shorts and a pair of black lacy knickers. Yikes! I roll them back up quickly and go to text K.

> *<Have found said items, will bring with me to swimming tonight, no probs>*

08:20
Chuckling about her knicks. She must be mortified, poor woman. Think I'd better give them back together with some other items – to alleviate the blow, as it were. I know she wants to borrow a book on kayaking, plus she wants an entry form for the upcoming Brownsea Island swim event, so perhaps I'll give the lot to her in one go.

19:00
Swim training.

It's a busy swim session and I can hardly see Katherine, who's in the lane next to me. It's a mass of white water, bubbles and fizz. I'm certain she can't see much of me either. There are too many swimmers in the pool some nights. I mean, how on earth are we expected to eye up the opposite sex properly when there are a dozen other people creating heavy swell-like conditions that hinder the underwater seascape? Where's the Bermuda Triangle when you need it?

20:05

I manage to get my timings right and we walk slowly from the poolside to the changing rooms together – all fifteen yards of it.

'I have some items for you.'

K is a little flustered as I hand over the bag. 'Oh, thank you and, er, I'm so sorry,' she says, while noticeably blushing.

She perks up when I start talking about a used sea kayak I may have located and asks hurriedly, 'Do you think we can go out for another paddle again soon? I'm free this Friday afternoon if you are? I won't have any children to worry about until at least four. Can you get any time off from your work?'

I'm both pleasantly surprised and oddly relieved.

'For sure, of course.' Putting up about as much resistance as Winnie the Pooh would on being asked whether he's game for a full pot of honey.

'Okay, if you're sure. Friday it is for paddling then!' she says, glowing. 'Same place, same time!'

20:15

Am I missing something here? I mean, I suppose I could have given a brusque 'no' to this Friday. Put my foot down and said *I'm very sorry, I am unable to take you out because I'm a very busy man, I've a great deal of work on, I have a lovely girlfriend and you are married and you have three children, and I think you could spell big, big trouble!*

But I *do not have it within me* to turn her down. There is just *too much* excitement energising my body when I am in her company. It's as if I'm being driven by someone else who is in control of the steering wheel – and the accelerator but who is yet to find the means to operate the brake pedal!

JULY

'The more you give, the more I want to take...'

Friday 2nd July

13:10
Precipitation probability 0%. +24°
K forecast: ↑↑
Office forecast: ←→
Exercise outlook: ↑

I'm running late and cursing. Bloody traffic. I weave my way around slow moving cars and drive a lot faster than I should through the heath.

'Don't you know I've got a very important appointment? She's the most beautiful woman in the world and she's waiting for me!'

I turn into the parking area ten minutes late. I spy K standing next to her car and feel a whoosh of excitement run the length of my body.

She sees me. Oh, her eyes dissolve me on the spot. If ever Medusa had a beautiful sister, with body-melting powers, it's K. I sit like putty, unable to move until there's a tap on the window and she's mouthing, 'You okay?'

I come to, hop out, apologise for being late and start talking time frames. The most important thing on my mind is, how long have I got with this woman?

'Ninety minutes? Enough to get to Arne and back. What do you reckon?' I ask.

'Yes, where we went was lovely. Perhaps we could sit on the beach again?'

Oh yes, sit on the beach and chat. Discuss what you have been doing to me these past weeks. Sounds bloody perfect, I say to myself.

We head off, K leading eagerly in front while I place my boat just off her stern within chatting distance. K is on a mission, paddling at a high cadence into the short choppy conditions, which forces spray back along the length of the boat, and up into her face and hair.

Arne is more sheltered; the conditions are often more tranquil. Suddenly K is surprised by two grey seals who peek their heads up right in front of her boat.

'What? Look!' she says in a stage whisper, and points with her paddle to the pair of Labrador-like faces that are staring straight back at her.

I stop paddling and let my boat drift with the current as first one head disappears, then the other, only to reappear a few moments later thirty metres away, but this time on the other side of K's boat. 'How do they get there so quickly?' she asks. 'Are there any more of them?'

'Let's go and take a peek.'

It looks like the seals are in a playful mood, so we paddle gently over towards them and are able to get within a few metres before they vanish under the surface, but one of them – the smaller of the two – pops up its head again almost immediately and is no more than a metre from K's boat. It stares directly at her with its big, round, infinitely black eyes.

'I think this must be a youngster,' she says. 'He's quite small, but he seems so interested in *me*.'

Huh, can you blame him? I mumble to myself. *Sorry, Mr Grey Seal, I've got first shout. Okay?*

We follow the seals further up the channel and they seem content to swim around the boats from one side to the other underwater, as if it's a game of hide-and-seek.

K is loving the moment, as am I. If this is what being in heaven feels like, then it is a place I have no concerns about making a future reservation for.

'I think we should begin to head back. The tide is turning, it's low-water shortly and we will have it against us on the way back.'

'Okay,' she says. 'What time do you think it is now?'

'Not sure, but it will take us much longer than it did getting over, so we should head *thataway*.' I point towards Lake Pier.

'Will we have time to sit on our beach?'

My ears prick up when I hear the words 'our beach'. Our beach? Now, there's a proprietorial term if I've ever heard one, and I immediately feel a sensation of warmth deep in my chest.

The tide is running fast now, and our progress is slow. Once the harbour makes up its mind to empty itself, it can do so rather quickly, and we struggle to make it to our beach in reasonable time. K looks over to me with eyes that say 'we're not going to be able to stop' as we paddle past, and I nod. Thirty minutes later, we're finally back on the launch beach but I know we've been out much longer than originally planned.

'I'll check the time,' I say, running towards the car.

'Oops! It's nearly 3.30pm now,' I tell K.

'I'd better make a quick phone call.' She dashes off to use her mobile.

A little while later she reappears.

'All sorted, panic over. My neighbour is going to pick the children up… and she's going to feed them too, so there's no need to rush now.'

'In that case, why don't we go and get a cup of tea somewhere? The café at the park should be open,' I suggest.

'Or why not head back via my house? The tea will be better, and I have your book on kayaking that I've now read.'

I look at her a little startled and then after thinking about it for a few seconds simply respond with, 'That would be just perfect. I'll follow you back then.'

Oh shit! What am I doing now?

I'm driving but my mind is not on the road. I'm in convoy with one other vehicle, staring at the black car right in front of me and the person at the wheel. I can see intermittently, when the angle of the sun allows, occasional glimpses of the driver: the outline of the back of her head, her hair and the tops of her bare shoulders. At road junctions I'm treated to greater things as she turns her head to look left or to look right and I am given a wonderful profile of her face. For a few short seconds I can relish with uninhibited enthusiasm the delicate outline of her forehead, nose, cheeks, mouth and chin. I feel like an explorer discovering incrementally more than they could ever have wished for.

My stomach is a filled-to-capacity lepidopterarium as I try to arrive at a reasoned appraisal of the situation: I'm travelling back to K's house for a cup of tea. Sounds normal and is the perfect opportunity to have a proper chat with her. And what is wrong with that? But what if K's husband is there? Could be awkward. But why should it be? I've not done anything wrong, have I? What would I say to him? 'Hello, I'm the chap who's taken your wife out kayaking a few times, how do you do?' Nothing too much wrong with that – on the surface anyway. No, it'll be fine and if he should be there, I can be pleasant, polite and maybe even chat about his classic cars.

What if he's not there at first, but turns up while we are having tea? That could be more awkward. Not ideal for K either, I would have thought.

No, K would not invite me back to her house if Tim was going to be there. She just wouldn't do that. I'm sure I know her well enough now to know that it's not the sort of thing she'd do. Perhaps I don't know her that well at all and there's a slightly perverted streak to her character that I've not detected. Perhaps she likes to see others wallow in a sea of social discomfort? But *nothing has happened* I reassure myself. All I want to do is have a chat with K and try to understand where she is coming from and where I stand. I don't actually know she *likes* me. So why am I nervous? Okay, I fancy the heck out of her and a few odd inexplicable things have happened between us. But they could be coincidental. *Stop panicking*!

We arrive, and by the time I've clambered out of my car I can see the front door is already open. I can hear clattering in the kitchen as I tread gingerly into the porch.

'Hello?'

'In the back here, in the kitchen,' K calls. I walk along the high-ceilinged hallway to see her standing at the sink filling the kettle.

'Nice house.'

'Yes, thank you. A bit different from our last place. We've always wanted to live here. The mortgage is huge, but the house is ideal. The children each have their own bedroom, so no more sharing!'

The big house is silent as I move to the kitchen window and peer through encroaching vines.

'The garden looks amazing. Bet it keeps you busy?'

'Yes, it does, but I love my garden. I could spend all my time out there. It's a bit of a mess at the moment, everything is growing so fast.'

'You have green fingers then? I somehow thought you might,' I say, clumsily answering my own question. 'You are in possession of many gifts.'

We both peer through the window as K points out to me the names of some of the smaller trees and shrubs and gives a run-through of the plants flowering in the numerous pots scattered over the terrace. I listen to her obvious passion, finding it adorable.

'What's in the shed?' I ask, pointing to an old red brick building near the house. 'It looks like an old boiler house or coal house.'

'Ah, that is now Tim's photographic shed. He's converted it so that he can develop and print his black-and-white photography. It's a big thing with him.'

'Nice shed. A man's got to have a shed.'

'Well, he's got a few and the garages are full of his stuff.'

'Where do you keep your things?'

'I don't really have much, just a few chairs, and that table over there is mine,' she laughs. 'I don't really feel the need to own many possessions, never have done. I've a very good racing bike and I would like a nice sea kayak—'

There's a noticeable glint in her eye.

'Er, right. Okay, I'm working on it. I'll find something suitable for you.'

I sense it's the right time to ask about something that has been bugging me for the past hour. I query as casually as possible, 'So Tim, at work, is he?'

'Yep, he won't be back for ages yet. He works late on Fridays. I'll need to pick up the children at some stage. Earl Grey all right?'

And with that, the considerably weighty barbell is lifted from my chest and I feel kilograms lighter instantly.

I move to the back of the kitchen and prop myself up on the sideboard while K picks up the boiling kettle from the Aga. I take a quick look around and spy a smart radio on the windowsill, children's paintings on the wall, loose photos pinned haphazardly to a corkboard, a 2004 calendar with copious notes in different handwriting on the back of the kitchen door, a box of broken crayons and a colouring book on the sideboard, someone's teddy with half an arm missing, and by the larder a large wooden box of fresh vegetables, marked 'organic produce'.

'Take a seat,' K offers, but I'm happy to stand. The last few minutes have been revealing but also confusing. Too much talk of 'us' and 'we' and it's not the 'us' and 'we' I'd like it to be. I'm standing in a large, imposing house of an obviously successful man. With his wife who I am hugely drawn to. And I have a girlfriend and I'm quite happy really and, oh! I don't know what is going on. What exactly is going on?

K hands me my mug of tea and moves back slowly to the side of the Aga. Very slowly. Too languid a pace for it to be considered normal. I stare at my mug, not wanting to make eye contact. But I know instinctively she is looking at mine. She's only a few feet away, no distance at all in the scheme of things, and slowly, inevitably, I capitulate. I am forced to look up and to meet those achingly beautiful oceans of blue. They are communicating in a language I've never encountered before and for an infinitesimal fraction of time, which may in fact have lasted as long as the age of the Universe, our eyes engage. She has unzipped me, undressed me, then re-zipped and redressed me and now she is eternally inside of me. From within, something that was in her has crossed an unknowable divide that separates our souls, unerringly finding its way deep inside me.

My right leg is quivering, and I brace it against the sideboard. My hands are gripping the wooden worktop edge so tightly, I can feel it whimpering. My reaction is to retreat. This is uncharted territory and I'm in unknown, dangerous waters. I need a safe path home.

And yet, I cannot leave. The urge to remain is powerful and I recognise K does not want me to go. She continues to stare into my eyes. There is an intensity to her gaze while her stance is open and inviting. I have to know, for perhaps only once, I have to know what it would be like to hold her. What would it be like to have my arms around her? How would it *feeeel*?

Yet, an insistent nagging part of my brain keeps urging *retreat*!

But – I can't control the urge a moment longer. I put out my arms and, in an instant, K slots into me like the missing piece of a jigsaw puzzle that's finally been found. A piece, honed to the finest engineering tolerances, that now fits effortlessly into its rightful position.

I clasp her firmly to my chest while her head nestles neatly beneath my chin, her arms tightly bound around my back. The effect is to drain every last ounce of energy from me. Suddenly, I feel hopelessly weak, but then, equally as quickly, I'm recharged, or, more accurately, given a new type of energy – Katherine energy, K-ness – that supersaturates my body, nourishing it, making me feel reborn and puissant.

We stand in silence, holding each other, absorbing the shared feeling for as long as possible, and then I gently kiss the top of her head. My lips brush a cushion of soft sweet-smelling brown hair and I am back to that heavenly place once more. We grip one another so tightly I can feel her heartbeat pummelling my chest. We rock gently like two boats riding up and over waves in unison.

Reluctantly – and for no apparent reason – our mutual grip loosens. My arms drop lazily down the curve of her back and over her hips, to gently meet her hands as we pull apart, our fingertips brushing against one another as we slowly separate.

Without saying a word and with my face looking away from hers, in fear of being caught in the glare of those all-conquering eyes once again, I turn half-heartedly and walk out through the kitchen door and away along the hall, not daring to look back. Should I turn and look I know I will want to go back inside, and everything will become completely *out of control*. For I don't think I have it in me to stop myself from pushing her to the carpet, ripping off her thin cotton summer dress, pulling aside those black lacy knickers and making intense, passionate, irrevocable love to her – on the kitchen floor.

17:45

I'm as high as the proverbial kite and grinning so much my cheeks ache.

About ten minutes away from home, I pull the car over into a layby, dig out my phone and type the words:

<Now I am never going to want to stop holding you...>

and press the Send button.

I turn the phone off. It's been a hugely emotional and unforgettable day. I have Lois staying with me this weekend and I need to gather myself together. And quickly.

Saturday 3rd July

11:10
Drizzle +15° Tour de France starts
Office: Closed
Bedroom exercise: ↑
Exercise outlook: See above

We're still in bed. The weather is rubbish and Lois doesn't do rain, so we've not ventured much further than the fridge and back. Lois is shocked at how cold it is and thinks we should relocate to Greece or Spain where the sun never stops shining – apparently.

I keep telling her that the weather has been incredible while she's been away, and this is the first rain that there has been for weeks. She doesn't believe me, even though my tee-shirt tan lines prove otherwise.

I've not seen Lois in weeks, and it *is* good to see her. We've lots to catch up on. She's still badgering me about a summer holiday. I'm trying to convince her that we shouldn't bother but go for a longer ski holiday this winter. She's warming to the idea, particularly as skiing is something she excels at.

Yesterday seems a long, long time ago, but my emotions are still in turmoil. I've relentlessly pushed K to the back of my mind – until after the weekend at least. K knows Lois is here, so it's a timeout. I'm enjoying my interregnum with Lois, living purely in and for the moment.

15:00
We should get up, but Lois insists on repeatedly exhausting me.

16:45
I am competing tomorrow, a twelve-mile sea kayak race in Cornwall, but at this rate Lois will have to do all the driving. And the racing too!

Monday 5th July

09:30
Grey, F4-5 +17°
Office forecast: Open
Training forecast: A bit pooped out. Got second place though!
Lois has just left. We didn't get back until late, but we were both up early as we have a busy week ahead. She's probably coming over again next weekend.

09:45
So, finally, I get time to myself and can let the dam burst. K comes rushing inland; it feels bloody fantastic! Ah, the relief, the relief to be at liberty to concentrate on her and her alone! I atomise time and relive each tiny particle of Friday afternoon. Luxuriating in the sensation of finally having her in my arms, and oh, my… *the difference.*

10:10
Will she be at swim training tonight? I'm guessing yes, but since we never got a chance to talk at the weekend, it would be good to know.

10:30
Perhaps I should text her. Check she is okay. Ask if she is going to be there. Maybe we can get ten minutes together?

10:45
Finding it difficult to concentrate. I need to know how she is. I need to know what is going on. I need to know all sorts of things, but most important of all, I need to see her.

11:05

<Would like to see you>

I think she's as troubled as I am. How brilliant is that!

<Would like to see you too. U swimming?>

<Yes. See u there>

Thank God. I can relax now, well, for the rest of the day anyway.

19:00

Swim training.

'Right, you miserable lot, we're doing some long sets, all front crawl. Eight times two hundred metres and four times two hundred metres. Your target times are on the board. Let's get to it,' barks Mark.

To be honest, I don't feel like flogging myself – particularly after yesterday's race. My shoulders ache and I'm not in the mood to go fast. The only positive thing is that K and I can play our game underwater again. I look over to her in the next lane and she's grinning at me.

I've wimped out from leading the lane and Big Roy takes on the responsibility. I'm sitting on his toes getting a nice tow. K has also gone off number two in her lane, so over the course of the set we should run parallel to one another at some point and get a chance to do our synchro thing at the turns.

It's taken a few lengths to get our timing right but, on the last turn, we nailed it. Trouble was, we were laughing so much I started to drown and had to pull over to let the others pass.

We try again on the next set and it sort of works, but then K gets the giggles and comes up short, out of breath and gasping for air. By the final set, we've got it together and our childish game keeps us entertained until the end of the session. Our overall times are faster than we expect.

I make sure I'm right next to K, but, as is quite usual, people stand about in the pool chatting. I can see K is waiting for me. She hops out from the pool and is ready to walk to the changing rooms. Time contracts and I know I only have a few metres' worth of talking time before she disappears, so I make my excuses and hurriedly pull myself out of the water.

'Can you meet for coffee?' I ask, without preamble. 'Tomorrow morning?'

'Yes. What time?'

'Eleven o'clock. Bella's Café. You know it?'

'Yes.'

A short but vital conversation.

Tomorrow then. We will be able to talk, discuss, deliberate, review, thrash out whatever the bloody hell is going on between us!

Tuesday 6th July

11:00
+19°

'Out of her looks into my vitals came'
(P.B Shelley 1792–1822)

Bella's café.

Can one look say it all? Yes, it most certainly can. In one quick, penetrating azure-blue glance, I get confirmation of what I've been unconsciously yearning for – for what seems like a lifetime. She is in a place as messy, whisked-up and frenetically chaotic as I am. It's a form of mutual pandemonium.

We choose a table by the window in the far corner looking over the sea and at the Purbeck hills. I sit down opposite K on inopportune squeaky vinyl cushions and, as our knees bump together, she smiles but remains entirely silent.

The waitress asks what we'd like, and I order, presumptuously, a pot of Earl Grey tea for two.

We try talking – polite, unimportant stuff. It is useless. The conversation fizzles out. We both stare into space. I fiddle too much with the sugar shaker. K turns from the sea view and concentrates her look on me as if to say *the time is right*. I am at liberty to ask – to ask the question that has plagued me since the moment I first laid eyes on her. Since I first encountered the woman who gives me scientifically inexplicable electric shocks along with countless sleepless nights. Can it only be five weeks since my life was upended?

So I say, 'I cannot stop thinking about you. About what you have *done* to me… and *what* you are *doing* to me.'

K lowers her head, breathes in deeply, then looks up and returns my gaze, saying quietly, 'Shit! It's the very same for me. I was hoping that it was just *me* who felt like this, but you do too? *Oh no*!'

She pauses for a moment, then assertively, says, 'What the *bloody hell* are we going to do now?'

Wednesday 7th July

10:20

*Sunny lovely, brown feet

Finally slept last night. There is relief tempered with uncertainty. Relief she has the same feelings for me as I for her. It leaves me euphoric. But the potential life-disruption for all involved and impossible-to-imagine future is like walking close to the edge of Burning Cliff in a roaring south-westerly.

Thursday 8th July

09:30

I've begun drafting a letter to K. Started it yesterday but the problem is I can't decipher much of what I wrote in my notepad – during a stream-of-consciousness frenetic download – while out and about. No matter, I'll give it another go later.

09:45

Just spoken to Lois. Tactfully explained that seeing her Sunday is now out as, under peer pressure, I've just officially entered the annual pier-to-pier swim between Bournemouth and Boscombe. I've done it the last few years and it's nothing too serious. A fun social event as much as anything. Deep down, I'm hoping I can persuade K to join me. I know she'll want to do the race; it is just whether she can free herself. I'll mention it tonight at swimming.

Friday 9th July

10:30
Lance Armstrong is leading the Tour again
Office forecast: ↑
Exercise outlook: ↑

Almost finished the first page of the letter to K. Tempted to have a go at doing something else for her as well, but not sure yet.

11:15
Text from K.

> *<Hoping I can do Sunday. Have two children sorted, third one still pending! Can't swim tomorrow...>*

> *<OKs. Understand>*

As I hit the Send button, I realise what I've just said. Understand? Do I really understand anything? What can it be like trying to juggle three young kids when you want to go out and play yourself? What's Tim doing? I've not dared discuss her family's dynamics, but I'm impressed by how K manages to juggle so many balls. As for my 'understanding', well, what experience have I got of any of this? Nowt! A big round zero.

Sunday 11th July

10:30

Blue. F2-3 SW, hot +26°, Water temp +14°

<Might be late for start. Don't wait for me!>

K's on her way and I'm just about to head down to sign on for the race. She might just make it if the start is delayed – which it often is.

Despite recent weeks of sunshine, the water is far from warm. That said, I am wearing a lightweight racing neoprene suit, as are many others. Okay, so it is not such 'pure' open water swimming as wearing only a cossie, but the thin neoprene keeps you warm, and I happen to think that's more important.

The race is about to start, and I search anxiously for K. The mass of swimmers in the water, all wearing the same coloured hats, makes it tricky to pick anyone out – even K.

The horn sounds and we're off! There's a great deal of splashing and arms and legs flaying everywhere, but I manage to get onto the feet of some chap who is swimming quite rapidly and we gradually pull clear of the confusion and find less disturbed water. I hang onto his wake – just. Gritting my teeth. I'm not going to be able to get past him and I hope he can see where he's going, because I can't! Even though there are no corners in this event, it's very easy to end up weaving and to lose time. Navigation in a straight line is vital. But my tug seems to have his bearings sorted and twenty-nine minutes later we both exit the water at the finish line. We jog up the beach together, although I maintain a respectful distance behind him, to the applause of the crowd.

I look back to the mass of bobbing heads and try to pick out K again. She has such a distinctive front crawl that's quite wide but with a relaxed arm recovery – like a seagull wing, and it looks so very graceful.

I think I see her, leading a group who are sitting on her feet getting a tow and, sure enough, as the group gets closer, I spy her coming ashore through the slight surf.

She sits on the beach recovering, but she's still not seen me. I go over to her, bend down by her side and say, 'Excuse me, would you like a cup of tea?' She looks up, laughs joyously and takes the cup slowly from my hand. Our fingers brush lightly as she does so.

'I was trying to find you at the start, but I was late. Where did you finish?'

'Didn't win, but that's okay. Some young lad led the way for me! But you did really well, considering you started at the back.'

'I got held up a bit early on but once I could see where I was heading, I really enjoyed it. It's so refreshing swimming in the sea, I love it.'

'Can you hang around for a bit or do you have to shoot straight off?'

'Nope, I'm free now till four o'clock! It's all sorted. With the weather like this, do you fancy going over on the ferry to Studland beach? We could hang around there.' It's clear she's excited at the prospect.

'You're on. I'll meet you back at the start point then. Race you there?'

'There's a challenge! I'll jog along the beach, you can swim. Last one back buys the ice creams!'

I dive back into the sea and re-swim the course while trying to keep my eye out for K, who's jogging slowly back along the shoreline.

The tide has started to turn now, and I can feel it working against me. What felt comparatively easy half an hour ago is now draining. Quickly, my limbs are starting to ache. So much for all my bravado – perhaps I should have chosen the land option.

Some considerable time later I stroll out from the water's edge trying to look entirely relaxed – although, in fact, all I want to do is collapse onto the sand and gasp like a landed mackerel. I see K standing high on the beach wall with her arms folded – clearly amused at my distress. I semi-jog over, and we compare notes. I tell her how incredibly tough the conditions were and how I had to contend with two massive Great Whites and a barracuda that would not let go of my leg. 'So, all things considered,' I say, 'I think I did rather well.'

We walk the short distance back up to the Overcliff car park and our moods change as we leave the hustle and noise of the beach behind. Up here, on the cliffs overlooking Bournemouth's golden beaches that stretch for miles in either direction, there is solitude.

'So, we have until four o'clock. That's fantastic.'

K is looking at me and seems to purr. She holds out her hand and encourages me to climb onto a park bench to get a better view of the scene below. I take her hand and instinctively thrust K in front of me. I wrap my arms around her from behind. She clasps my hands over her middle and pushes gently back into me; my chin rests on the top of her head and ever-so-swirly hair that every now and then flies into my face stirred by the clifftop breeze. There's a fragrance of the salty sea, fresh air and K that is unendurably arousing. I squeeze her even more tightly. *Nothing can surpass this, nothing*, I say to myself.

But, all too quickly, things are brought to a rude halt. A loud yell, directed towards us it seems, forces us to rapidly disengage. We turn to see what the commotion is, half expecting it to be someone we know; instead, and thankfully, it's nothing more than an irate dog walker berating his runaway hound.

I turn to K. 'We must be careful you know. We can't afford to be seen together like this, not here.'

K nods.

'C'mon let's get over to Studland. It'll be quieter over there, less chance of being spotted and we can lose ourselves in the sand dunes.'

'Yup, you're right. Let's get going.'

We grab our things, jump into my car and head down to the chain ferry and towards the long white and wonderfully soft sandy beach.

20:15

Home.

My left hand feels naked. And I am no longer the same man because of it. K has a power over me that I don't understand and, if I am honest with myself, scares me witless. When we are physically connected, when our fingers are interlaced, palm on palm, skin on skin, there is a life force that flows down through her arms, through her hands, through her fingertips and into mine. It is an energy that is utterly vibrant and vital. It's as if she is communicating with me on some profound physical, non-verbal level. Right now, I am convinced her fingers were only ever designed to fit inside of mine.

And as I write this, and now that K is no longer connected to me, my body feels so bereft and hollow, it could echo.

20:20

Have sent a text to Lois to say that I'll be over first thing in the morning. I can't face driving to her house tonight.

Tuesday 13th July

07:15
Sunshine open, hot, hot +28°
Office forecast: READY

It's early and I'm trying to get home from Lois's before the traffic builds. I'm behind on so many work things it's embarrassing. Graham is on my case – big time. And all I want to do is finish my letter to K.

11:15
Text from K.

<*Are you free this eve? Have something for you…*>

Yesterday was tough, having to box her up and throw away the key again for twenty-four hours, and Sunday seems like an age ago.

<*Yes. Where + when? I have something for you too!*>

<*Only have about thirty mins free tonight. 9pm Old Barn pub?*>

<*OKs. See u there*>

20:50

'And odours warm and fresh fell from her hair'
(P.B Shelley)

It's a glorious summer evening. Dorset is clothed in all its finery and on its best behaviour. I order two glasses of merlot and wander out into the pub garden. I find a wooden bench and twist it around so that it faces the late evening sun. In my pocket is a white envelope. An hour ago I had nothing but crumpled pieces of paper adorned with more hieroglyphics than Tutankhamen's tomb, but after some frantic deciphering, that would have made Alan Turing proud, I have a finished letter ready to place into the hands of the woman I am waiting for.

I hear a car pull into the car park. K is walking briskly towards the pub wearing a sky-blue sleeveless cotton dress that highlights her Americano coffee-coloured tanned skin. Her luxurious brown hair is sun streaked – like racing stripes – and is pinned in place by a tortoiseshell-coloured hair clip.

I stand to greet her and as I do, she pushes a dark green envelope into my hand. 'This is for you,' she says, brooking no argument and sitting down beside me. She appears a little flustered.

I give her the glass of wine, but she immediately says, 'I don't have long. Please don't ask how I've managed to get away this evening.'

'I won't. Don't risk getting into trouble. Okay?' I pause. 'I am *very pleased* to see you.'

I lift her hand, kiss it, and gently put it in mine. I squeeze it tightly. Our fingers eagerly align, and I can feel her relax immediately. She sighs.

'You've written me a letter?' I ask.

'Yes. But you mustn't read it now. It's for later.'

'Later when?'

'Later, it's for later, for when you're on your own.'

'It's not bad news is it?'

'No, definitely nothing like that.'

The sun is dropping and is obscured by the trees now, so I suggest we move the bench a few feet to a remaining patch of sunlight. We settle again.

'I have something for you too.'

'Really? What?'

'I have also written a letter!'

We laugh.

'Read it to me then.' She is impatient.

'No! If it is forbidden for me to read your letter to me, then I won't read mine to you aloud!'

She thinks for a moment.

'I'm really embarrassed. You read your letter to me first.'

'No, you first,' I insist.

'No, you go first.'

'Very well. I'll read your letter – aloud.'

'No. You read yours and I'll read mine. But you first.' Now she's smiling broadly.

'Agreed. But I have to tell you that mine is in two parts. The first is a letter and the second is a poem, of sorts anyway. But you must not laugh, or I'll never be able to write one again – ever!'

'A poem?'

'Oh yes!' she says excitedly. She laughs again, perhaps too loudly, adding to my already pressured state.

'But you must read yours out before I read my two pieces,' I say. 'New rules.'

'Alright,' K agrees. 'I'll read mine out now, but let me have a drink first. Here goes.'

(Monday in the sunshine)

Dear Whoeveryouare,

What are you doing to me? I feel and look like I've been hung!

Nervous energy continually robs me of previously taken for granted contentment. I can't sit, eat or sleep. Too many frightening thoughts preparing future memories and scaring myself silly. At the moment, I could swim all the way around Brownsea Island doing just doggy paddle. The only thing that isn't improving over time is the amount of sleep I'm getting. To be honest, I don't know how I'm still standing.

Time is now a miserable commodity. When we're together there's simply isn't enough and at all other times far too much! And it's NOT enough! I really thought we could get it out of our systems somehow. Spend a little bit of time together, satisfy the need, do some watery activities and then go our separate ways once the immediate urgency of our attraction was quenched. And then... be happy in our prosaic lives. But NO! The more you give... the more I want to take.

This morning I was browsing a second-hand bookstall when my phone vibrated and it was you. I quickly paid the 60p for the book before answering the phone. Imagine my gasp (audible) when I opened (at any page) and read:

'There's never any knowing – how am I to put it – which of our actions, which of our idlenesses won't have things hanging on it forever.'

Strangely, prophetic words now jump out at me from every page and every song. I'll sprinkle some on you from time to time... unless you're not the deeply poetic man I think you are?

Sometime hence, when all is as it should be, try to get hold of E. E. Cummings' 'Somewhere I have never travelled, gladly beyond.' It's the most beautiful poem but now is not the right time to share it with you. Too much, too soon.

I'm very frightened, a bit sad... and quite confused, but amazingly, when on those waves and in the water with my guardian angel beside me... everything is just perfect!

And... you, you are such a gentleman and have never taken any liberties as it were. The other afternoon – in the kitchen at home – I take all responsibility. You could have done more –

on multiple occasions – and I thank you for that… for where would we be now? Do you think we have set those boundaries? I'll push so you must push back – I owe it to my family. You said so yourself.

But… I am happy to go with this for now, let's see where it takes us…

PS. Memories of Studland last Sunday and your gentle manly moments – (whiter than the rest):

You in your swimwear on the beach, having emerged from the sea (like the Milk Tray man) just to be with me.

The warmth as we lay among the sand dunes (the sun's rays were weak in comparison).

Holding hands.

The consideration you show me, always. To be treated as you treat me means more than you know. (It is normally me teetering on the outside edge of a pavement, dicing with road death to protect others, and you do it so effortlessly.)

The realisation that we fit! Your chest is just the right size for my head and my shoulders fit snugly under your arm.

But best of all, was the journey back along Studland beach to the ferry. I don't think we said anything. We just were.

'*Holy shit*! That is *some* letter,' I say.

'I wanted to write more, but… anyway. You read yours now, *please*.'

'Righto. Big breath, here goes. It's the letter part first, then the poem. Remember, no bloody laughing!'

I pull out the envelope, smooth out the two pieces of paper, take an extra-large gulp of wine, and begin:

Tuesday + other days too…

Dear 'Person I've Only Known For 42 (approx) Days',

Quite what has happened in the last five weeks I just don't know! How does a five foot four inch brown haired blue-eyed woman, who is married with three children, stroll so casually and catastrophically into my life? How does someone tear a hole in my psyche and reach inside – into my soul – having done little other hitherto than exist! What forces are in operation?

You should know that throughout this time I have been searching desperately to find fault! Yes! Something… anything that will be a reason, an excuse even, to allow me to pull away from you. So I can say, 'Nah, she's not much cop really, nothing in common, a bit too bossy for me etc, etc.' But the more I am shown, the more I find perfection and the more of you I desire! Why can't you be in possession of a few characteristics that are really off-putting!!

I feel I know a great deal about you and what you desire and I believe you feel the same for me. Our connection of familiarity is overwhelmingly wonderfully scary!

You are so stunningly beautiful. And I am not the only one to have noticed. You have earnt a fan club among the male component of the swimming group (I cannot comment on how the females feel!) I could write pages galore about your beauty, but for now I shall restrain myself. Soon, however, I will sit and talk with you of your natural beauty (when the moment is right) and relish your blushes.

Trying not to touch you has been difficult. At the Regatta, when I accidentally touched the top of your leg, so much heat was transmitted in an instant I almost burned (electric shock aside). Ever since, I've wanted to repeat the experience but have made considerable efforts to avoid it. I ache to touch your hand, a simple caress so your magical energy will flow into me. I'm certain I sense your soul.

For many sleepless nights I have fantasised about wrapping my arms around you – holding you tightly and absorbing the whole of you... living within your aura, in touch with your every breath and movement, everything: your smell, your breath, your warmth... your... unique youness!

I have not experienced anything like this before – seduced and entranced so quickly, so powerfully and so effortlessly. Will it diminish? Dissolve and dilute like an ink drop in running water? I hope not. Like two stars, we have met and collided in a big explosion and... well... what now? There must be a prevailing universal reason why two people have connected so profoundly. I pray it will not be the case. I know I can be entirely honest with you, indeed any attempt to be dishonest is an absolute impossibility, the power you have over me. No matter how trivial a thing, I am obliged to share it with you. I want you to experience everything I experience. I want to be wherever you want to be. My barriers are collapsing and the sunlight is finally invading my soul.

I finally feel a somebody.

There's a long silence. An unearthly stillness descends as if the world-above is holding its breath. Until K breaks the spell.

'Read me your poem,' she says simply.

so natural

she is
the most beautiful woman i have ever seen
in this world, so natural and untainted,
blemished not by the ravages of this life
so complicated.
she wears no plastic about her person.

goodness flows
like nectar'd-scented rain whatever

the storm, and kindness seeps from every pore
of her soft shell, so free of darkness
and i told-you-so's.
easily she gives her time – as far as i can tell.

listening words
pirouette from her lips and tumble
at a graceful pace, all manicured and assembled
and softness falls to those who hear the music
– can never forget.
serenity is her rostrum.

an aura
richer than the golden sands that wear our prints
envelops her fabric, so radiant and emanating,
no one other donates enthusiasm so imperviously –
indeed.
not just i see the beauty which she carries.

As I approach the end, my cheeks are damp with unsolicited tears. K is crying too. She grips my arm fiercely.

'How truly pathetic are we?' I rasp.

'Yes. We most certainly are,' she sobs. 'I can't believe how beautiful it is – and it's about me? Surely not.' She is whispering like an overwhelmed child.

'Please believe me – it is entirely about you. It is how I see you. This is how you are to me.'

I carefully brush the tears from K's cheeks, and we rest our heads together. I sit back briefly, then lean forward a fraction so our noses touch; we both smile at the sensation. I can hear her breathing becoming heavier and her chest is visibly rising and falling. I recognise it is time to kiss this woman. I have wanted to kiss her so badly and on so many occasions. And now, finally, the moment has arrived. I move my head to one side a little, K moves hers too – and our lips touch. We kiss, pressing hard into each other as my hand reaches around the back of her head, pulling her closer. K responds eagerly and I feel her pushing herself against me, forcing us even closer, if that were possible.

There is no influence that could be brought to bear that would stop our swollen kisses.

We continue taking the briefest moments to breathe. The night is descending, and it is only the late evening drop in temperature that prevents us from making the bench our bed for the night.

Eventually the subconscious parts of our brains signal that it is time to separate. Millimetre by millimetre we extract ourselves from our overpowering embrace. We stay fixed – forehead to forehead, eyes drowning in mutual inchoate deep rings of blue.

We hold on to the moment for as long as we can. Then K speaks.

'I don't want to go. I don't want to leave you. But I *must* get back.'

'Yes. I understand. You mustn't be late home.'

We stand together. K thrusts my letter into her bag, we kiss again hurriedly, and she turns to go.

'I'll text you tomorrow?' I shout.

'Yes, please do that. Of course. Yes, you should!'

Wednesday 14th July

10:30
+26°
K forecast: Blue, blue, blue. Sky is blue, blue, blue too!
Grin size: XXL
Exercise outlook: ↑

Slept like a baby! Out for nine hours and now I feel *alive*! The world from my window has taken on a different colour.

10:40
Kissing K last night was quite unbelievably fantastic but, strangely, I would say that when we held hands for the first time on the beach on Sunday it felt equally as intense and as passionate as kissing her lips. I didn't think that would be possible. Lips are sweet, butterscotch and juicy, while hands are bare and dry. How can a clasp of hands feel as intimate as the union of lips?

Will someone explain, please?

11:15
It's K.

<Last night... I so didn't want to leave your kissing lips>

Then.

11:16

<There's a hell of a good universe next door... let's go!>

11:20
I reply.

> *<There is no place better than with you by my side>*

Thursday 15th July

13:30
No complaints +28°
Grin size: XXL
Exercise outlook: ↑

It's been a slow morning so far. Have been trying to focus on work but really, I'm just circling over planet K. Waiting for swim training tonight.

15:30
Graham is hassling me for the next quarter sales projections – but I'm not motivated.

18:45
Swim training.

I am stood in a scruffy corridor that sits between two squash courts! It's the only place I can find that is hidden from casual view and has the advantage that it's easy to hear anyone coming along the narrow concrete walkway. It's not particularly salubrious but it is private.

K texted saying she'd try to arrive early so we could have a few minutes together.

18:50
Ah-ha! I hear some hurried footsteps which sound like flip-flops. I walk to the end of the passageway and stick my head around the corner. K beams the moment she sees my face. I melt. My heart accelerates

tenfold and there's a rush of life throughout my body. I wait until she's hidden from anyone's sight before I put out my arms towards her, and she's nestled securely in my chest before I know it. K lets out a long loud sigh.

An intake of scent, a joining of the lips, a look into her eyes… but just not for long enough. Holding her in my arms, she robs me of all my energy in the instant we combine but then somehow throws it all back to me with extra fizz and bubble. Energy somehow flows out-of-me-and-into-her-then-out-of-her-and-back-into-me at double-strength. She's a flippin' walking dynamo and I can't get enough!

'We're going to be late,' I say wretchedly. 'We ought to go.'

'Yes, I suppose so.' She slowly loosens her grip and lets her arms slide recalcitrantly down my back.

We kiss quickly, then walk back to the locker rooms with, I suspect, an over-exaggerated air of innocence.

20:55
Post swimming.

I'm walking back to my car after a hard session, feeling satisfyingly exhausted. My phone buzzes. It's K.

<Did you hear my heart pounding? Oh dear>

ONE DAY LATER

Saturday 17th July

11:15
+26°
After swimming.

Too many people at swim training today. The weather has brought them out. More of a pool party than a serious training session.

It's coffee time in the upstairs bar and everyone is chatting noisily – generally catching up or talking sport. Plenty of faces I've not seen here for a while.

K is in demand. She's perched up on one of the stools overlooking the pool surrounded by four men, while I'm at the other end of the bar. There is a crowd between us. Siobhan's penetrating shrill laughter knifes through the air, silencing everyone for a moment.

It's an oddly pleasant feeling to be part of a crowded room when the person you want to be with most is tantalisingly metres away. Our conspiratorial secrecy undoubtedly adds to the frisson.

I'm on the edge of K's gravitational pull. I feel a powerful urge to say something to her, but it's difficult to find an open path towards the heart of the sun.

In frustration, I grab a pen from my kit bag and, on the wrapper of an energy bar, write six words: *You make my life worth living.*

I drift in and around the middle of the room where K is now standing. She's the centre of a group, engrossed in conversation, and I nestle up behind her. I prod K's hip a couple of times with the bar. She turns and looks down to see my hand and takes the bar gently from my fingers.

For a few minutes we stand comfortably together as we satisfy a burning thirst, drinking in the lightest of physical contact, hip against hip, arm touching arm. No one else has any idea what's going on.

K recognises I need to speak to her and makes her excuses to the others. She must get back to make lunch for the kids, you know how it is. I explain I have an appointment with my computer and we both slip away.

'What have you given me?' she asks.

'Read the ingredients list. Read them later. But, don't give the bar away. Okay?'

'I won't.'

K dives into her kit bag and pulls out a cream-coloured envelope.

'I have something for you, too,' she says, smiling.

'Can I open it now?'

'Yes, definitely. Now.'

I open the envelope and pull out a card. A painting of a pair of courting mallard ducks, wings flapping.

'Wow! Beautiful,' I say.

'I saw it, liked it and knew you would too. Look on the reverse.'

I turn it over and, on the back in her perfect handwriting, she has written:

'for whatever we lose (like a you or a me)

it's only ourselves we find in the sea'

My lips move as I read the words, but quickly K interrupts in a serious-sounding voice, 'These are our words – *our words* – you must keep them!'

Slightly perplexed, I reply, 'Yes. Of course. Of course, I will. Thank you. I'll read them later.'

'Yes, make sure you do.'

She looks up at the hallway clock.

'I really do have to go. The children need feeding, as will Tim, and I've not prepared a thing yet!'

I move a little closer as if to kiss her but then think better of it. I step back and K runs her hand down the length of my back and into my hand. Without saying anything, we walk out into the bright sunshine and go our separate ways.

14:50

I've gone through my few poetry books trying to find who wrote the words on K's card – and, of course, it is E. E. Cummings. I should've guessed. I've read the poem '*maggie and milly and molly and may*' but still have no clear idea why K chose the two lines.

16:50

Text from K.

> *<Thank you for the much needed sustenance today (you + your words). But more needed soon pls. Monday?>*

> *<Yes, Monday more>*

Sunday 18th July

11:30
Annoyingly nice
Office forecast: ←→

I've been up since six am trying to get a business plan into shape. I've still a lot to do. And it looks lovely outside too. I wonder what K's up to today? Sunday is probably family day, I'm guessing. Lois is coming over later, so I need to change my mindset before she arrives.

Tuesday 20th July

09:30

I've decided I need to buy K a new mobile phone. I'm worried her current mobile, a work-provided phone, is too accessible. The number of texts we are now sending to each other makes it dangerous should someone (i.e. hubby Tim) pick it up or check the bill. I've suggested K delete our texts after she's read them, but I'm not entirely convinced she does.

Wednesday 21st July

08:45
F2-3 SW, hot +21°

<Bella's café 12.30?>

<Yes, seat by the window>

12:15
I'm hoping that K might arrive early. She's managed to get forty-five minutes free.

12:20
I have K's new mobile phone, bought this morning. It's a bit Fisher-Price but it'll do the job. I think she will approve of the idea. It looks very much like her existing work phone anyway. Do I give her it before I tell her about my week away with Lois or after? Not much of an advantage either way, really. Anyway, I just want to see K and hold her. Where is she?

12:30

<5 mins!>

12:35
The café door opens, abruptly followed by urgent footsteps across the wooden floor. I stand up in anticipation. We grab one another

forcefully, hold for not-enough-seconds, inhale one another deeply and then kiss. K sits opposite me. I hold her hand over the table and an immediate sense of rightness envelops us.

We discuss swimming. I urge her to enter the Brownsea Island sea swim in a few weeks' time and she's up for it. 'I can fill out the application form for you,' I say. 'I just need a few details – your full address and date of birth.'

She smiles. 'My date of birth? Really?'

'Yes, I can fib but it would be embarrassing to see you collecting the silverware for the Under twenty-ones!'

'Okay, I've nothing to hide! It's twenty-eighth August 1961.'

'You're kidding me. You're *older* than me! No, I don't believe you.'

Now I am laughing, and an elderly couple look over from their table, curious.

'How is that even possible?' I ask in a hushed voice, as if she's got a secret only for me. 'Have you been preserved in aspic for ten years or kept in the dark?'

'The latter, I think!'

'And there's me thinking I might be accused of cradle snatching.'

K squeezes my hand in a way that's in part intimate and part *please shut up now*. I get the message.

'Okay, I'll post the entries tonight and hope we both get in.'

I decide to give K her present.

'I've got you something,'

She looks excited.

'The clue is on the box,' I say.

'Oh… it's a phone.'

She looks a tad disappointed and a bit perplexed.

'Open it.'

'Ah, it's the same model and colour as mine.'

'Yes.'

I run through my idea quickly to explain. Then I watch as K's eyes light up. She has quickly worked out what this could mean.

'It's your hotline to the White House, and mine too. No one will ever know. Just make sure you keep the two phones in different places and this new one on vibrate mode only. I've already programmed in my two numbers for you. I'm listed as housekeeping.'

'Housekeeping? I like that. So, I can phone either one of the numbers and you'll come round and sort everything out for me?'

'That's the idea.'

'Well, I'm definitely going to be giving that a go, then. Expect no peace!' she whoops.

We fire up and test the phone. K pops it into her inside coat pocket and zips it up.

'It'll be safe in here, or I'll have it close to me in my knicks at all times! Thank you.'

'Give me the box and paperwork, so I can look after it,' I suggest.

'Yes, of course. Tim will only ask questions otherwise.'

I decide the time is right to tell her the less good news.

'I have something to tell you,' I say solemnly.

'Oh no, what is it?'

'I'm going away for a few days. In fact, for seven days.'

'What? When?'

'Tomorrow night. Back next Friday.'

'Oh no!' K is forlorn. 'Where are you going?'

'Spain, but I really don't want to go. You know why, right?'

K doesn't say anything, so I reach over and take her other hand from her lap and place it across the table. I gaze into her eyes and we smile sadly at one another.

'It's a week but I'll text you every day.'

'It might be easier to cope if we don't communicate. I will tell myself I'm not going to get excited for seven days,' K suggests, half-heartedly.

'Let's see,' I say resignedly. 'We'll take it one day at a time.'

Thursday 22nd July

16:30
Destination: Palma

I pull into Lois's driveway and from the kitchen window my ears are assailed by a blast of seriously naff Spanish music.

I cringe and must fight the urge to turn the car around and drive away. It's only seven days. Work worries can be parked; I can relax, enjoy warm weather training, soak up the Spanish sun and enjoy the company of Lois, my girlfriend. Yes, my girlfriend. Remember her?

What's my problem?

SEVEN DAYS LATER

Friday 30th July

14:30
Blue sky +27°
Back in Dorset. Thank God!

Yes, it was perfectly pleasant, and I've acquired a good suntan but lost quite a lot of fitness – not so good. Too many San Miguels, too many fantastic meals. Desperate to get back in my boat and in the pool – and desperate, so very desperate, to see K.

But I'm very nervous, and not sure entirely why. Part of me thinks she may have made an extra effort with Tim while I've been away. The past 192 hours have made her realise how much she and Tim are diverging and the best course of action is to have nothing more to do with me (please, God, no!). Or K may think, because I've spent the past 192 hours with Lois, I have changed my mind and don't want anything more to do with her (please, God, no!).

My last text to K, before I boarded the plane.

<Please wait for me>

I've only had one text from her since.

<Miserable>

So, I just don't know. Think I should text her and let her know I'm back.

<Back home. Spk?>

A little while later.

<At bloody last!!! Can't spk now. You swim tomorrow?>

<Yes>

Phew! She seems all right. But I'll be lucky to get any time alone with her on my own tomorrow. Saturday mornings are never easy.

Saturday 31st July

07:15
+25° Lance is going to win again!
K forecast: ↑ ↑
Tanned body: Tick
Training: ↑

I am feeling ridiculously nervous and have been up since six. I'm worried K is going to tell me she can't see me anymore because she's had time to *think* while I've been away. Who knows what crazy thoughts have been going through her head? I *should know* because crazy thoughts have been going through my head! Or perhaps the extraordinariness of our connection will have been dismantled by this brief, painful separation.

And I'm nervous because I'm also excited. Excited because I'm going to see K!

08:02
The lanes are rapidly filling with swimmers. Where is she?

I get going with the warm-up and, wow, the water feels heavy. It's very different from the clear seas off Cala Figuera. My body senses it is going to have to work today.

Now the warm-up is almost finished, and my heart has sunk to the bottom of the pool. She said she was going to be here, but where is she? I do the last four lengths on backstroke and it's a smart decision. I see K on the poolside coming out of the changing room; she's already spotted me. Her face lights up and she gives me her *look*. All my fears are ray-gunned. What a complete idiot I was to think things would be otherwise!

09:10

The session is finished, and I walk with K as slowly as possible along the poolside.

'Forget coffee,' she whispers. 'Meet outside in ten minutes.'

I nod my head in agreement.

One of the many things about K that makes me smile is the speed with which she can shower, change and be ready. It's a matter of minutes. Many women I know disappear into the changing room and that's it. Gone! As if swallowed by an other-worldly portal. If lucky, they reappear an hour or two later. What they do in there is a complete and utter mystery.

09:20

I'm loitering outside but K's has been caught by fellow swimmer, Ann.

09:25

At last! K is part skipping, part bouncing her way across the car park.

As she nears, she says, 'The quietest place I can think of is down at the churchyard.'

'Fine. There shouldn't be anyone we know around… except those few already under the ground. I'll see you among the headstones.'

09:35

In a far corner of the graveyard, a grieving widow has donated a sturdy bench that sits beneath a spreading Yew tree. It looks back towards the church and is tucked away. A perfect spot *to rest and be thankful*. K joins me. 'Do you think it is okay to sit here? To kiss and cuddle?' She laughs. 'We might be frowned upon – from both above *and* below.'

'I'm sure they'll be alright with it. But if the ground starts to shake, then yes, we better start running!'

We sit and K presses herself against me. I inhale her fragrance;

oh, how I have missed the smell of her skin and hair. I gently kiss her cheeks and forehead. 'It's been so painful,' I whisper.

K takes a deep, slow breath and I'm taken up with her. There's a momentary pause before she expels her breath and it's as if we are in free-fall.

'You cannot go away again,' she says. 'I have been so miserable. It has been unbearable.'

'I won't. I can't. I'm not going to again. It's been the same for me. The craving is too much.'

We sit back on the bench. K puts her legs onto my lap.

'I was late this morning because Tim suddenly announced he couldn't keep an eye on the children. He was being difficult. I think he's trying to prevent me from going swimming. He doesn't like me doing it.'

'Does he suspect anything?'

'I don't think so. He knows I've been agitated, particularly this last week, but no, I don't think he does. How is it with Lois?'

'When I'm with you I am at peace. Profoundly calm, tranquil and a feeling of complete oneness. Like now. There is *no better* sensation. With Lois it is very different. I hadn't noticed it before; I just accepted the way it was because that was all I knew. How does anyone know? Until one has actually tasted something so radically different, some exquisitely spiced appetite-satiating food, all one can do is believe in what one already has. But then your senses are reborn. With you, I suffer a constant desire to be always in your company. Once apart, my whole world turns grey, boring and painful. With you, everything is enlivened, a new gamut of colours I'd never have thought existed – they, you, illuminate my world and warm it up. It is beyond my imagining.'

'Do you find you have the urge to tell me the things you experience, no matter how trivial?' K enquires. 'I constantly wish I could tell you what I've been up to!'

'Yes, absolutely. I want to tell you about me and who I am and what I do on a minute-by-minute basis. If only I could. If only you were here all the time, I could really bore you to tears!'

We both laugh.

K looks at me questioningly. Her forehead furrows delightfully. Childlike.

'I've been meaning to ask, have you mentioned anything about me to anyone?'

'No, not directly. I would like to tell lots of people, including my family, but I've not revealed your name. I told my business partner I'd met someone 'special' but not elaborated. What about you?'

'I've tried not to, but I did say something to my dad last week. He asked me to be very careful. He would never tell anyone, not even my mum. We have a great relationship and I trust him implicitly.'

'We must be careful. You know what the swimming lot are like. It's gossip central.'

'We must. I can't afford anything to happen at the moment.'

The church clock strikes ten and K sits up as if she's about to leave.

'Do you have to go right now?' I ask.

'I'm okay for another fifteen minutes. I said I'd be back by half past.'

K rises and sits on my lap. I hold her tightly as she leans back into my chest. I rest my chin on the top of her head.

'You know it's the school holidays soon?' K says.

'No, I didn't. How's that going to affect things?'

'In the past Tim and I have taken it in turns to each have time with the kids. Individual mini-holidays – based around Tim's work schedule. Last night he suggested taking the three of them camping in the wagon for the first week. To Cornwall.'

'What? And you remain here?'

'Yes! I can't get time off from work until later in the month, so yes.'

'That means you might have more free time that week?'

'We're going to discuss it again tonight. I was going to tell you before you went away but I became deflated when I heard your news and—'

I kiss her on the cheek again with extra vigour and then we sit in a place of perfect stillness for a while, smiling.

10:15

We go our ways. As we must.

AUGUST

'One's not half two. It's two are halves of one'

Monday 2nd August

08:15

<Morning! Have a letter for u! Wrote it late last night. Don't take it too seriously. U swim?>

<Yes. See u at court #4. Usual spot>

<Tim is def going camping with kids next week>

<OKs! Discuss tonight>

18:40
Swim training.

'You must read this at home,' she says as she passes me a cream envelope with George written theatrically on the front. The words 'By Hand' appear in capital letters with two big exclamation marks in the top right corner. 'It was late last night, and I was thinking about things too much. It had been a long day. Anyway, there's not enough time to read it now.'

'Right.'

'Hold me?'

We embrace, clasped sculpture-like. Fixed while the world continues its indifferent orbit.

'So, what's the story with Tim, then?'

K takes her time to respond.

'He and the children are going to Cornwall for a week. They leave on Sunday. Robert and Michael want to go surfing. Anna didn't want to go with them at first but changed her mind. She hates being left out of anything.'

'You are working, aren't you? In whatever it is that you do.'

'Yes, next week part-time, then I'm finished completely for six weeks. Tim's only got two and a half weeks holiday this summer, so I'll be spending a lot of time with the children.'

'Does it mean I will be able to see more of you?'

'Yes, it does! Particularly next week.' K is laughing.

'I don't know what to say.'

'Say nothing.'

I lower my head and she pushes up onto her toes. We kiss, and with such intensity that other senses are dulled, negated. Gone are the cries from the squash courts behind us, so too the *thump-thump-thump* reverberations from the Body Pump class above. I'm in a world where any distraction is an offence against the new natural order of things. I want never to move from this here and now.

18:59

'We'd better get to the poolside or we will be missed,' K whispers.

'Yes, we probably should,' I say begrudgingly.

And with that, we pick up our kit bags and wander through to the big lane'd bath.

Tuesday 3rd August

07:20

I have a pint of builder's tea in my hand, I'm sitting on my garden bench overlooking 'the view' and have settled to read K's letter.

(Sunday late)

Dear Whoeverweare,

My version of the truth or the explanation for 'all this' (as I see it).

Keep in your mind, 'No man is an island entire of itself' and 'All Lose, Whole Find'. Think separateness = anxiety. Therefore, desire to connect.

If two people, who have been strangers, let the wall down between them and allow themselves to get close, that moment of oneness is the most exhilarating and exciting experience ever. As we know. But it is not unique. It ensures the continuation of the human race; it's why we are here.

These feelings we are experiencing (big time!) by their very nature do not last. Thank goodness. But they sometimes transform into something much more precious. This is what we don't know… yet? Anyway, there is a theory that the intensity of the infatuation is related to the degree of preceding loneliness – or separateness (cue John Donne).

We were obviously in the right place at the right time (or the wrong place at the wrong time, however you want to look at it). We both had a chasm that needed to be filled – may have been small in your case, a gulf in mine. I bet subconsciously we were looking for one another. I know which bit of me was missing. I can't speak for you, but if we felt some separateness, that explains the overwhelming desire to connect... and we do have many things in common.

But why the electricity, the heat, the pounding heart? If only we could enjoy each other's company without these physical symptoms (of malady!) how easy it would be to continue, or to stop! To be able to choose to do either! But with the added ingredient of explosive emotion, we have no choice. We are compelled to be swept along against all better judgement.

Like the strong tide in the harbour the other Sunday, rushing out of the entrance and stopping all the boats in their tracks, there is no paddling or swimming against it; it is too strong.

When does all this become – manageable?

Answers on a postcard please?

I've re-read the letter several times. K is keen to find a reason for the 'us'. My view is 'we just happened'. Fate works that way sometimes, so I'm happy to believe the reason for our meeting is 'beyond defining'. No point in over-thinking the reasons why. I'm excited to go along with it. As K says, I do not think we have much of a choice. It is becoming far too strong for us to resist. I feel the clock has been re-set.

07:40

I am working on another poem and letter.

Thursday 5th August

12:00
+19°
Training: ↑
Home office: ↑

I'm driving to Wareham to meet K for a pub lunch on the quay. Apparently, she's 'between visits' whatever that means. I've finished my new poem; cracked it last night – well, I think I have. It's not so much a poem, more a 'sitrep'. How things are right now, the state of play. I think K will like it as she's living in the same place as me, a place called Turmoil Land.

I also got the good news this morning that both our entries for Brownsea Island sea swim have been accepted. So, we're in! The downside is that it is in ten days' time, and I haven't been for a sea swim in weeks. K's not been in much either.

We'll go together next week.

12:15
She's early.

K hasn't seen me. She's sitting on one of the long wooden pews beneath the mullioned window. Her legs are tucked up beneath her and she's leaning against the aged wooden panelling. She sits in the welcome shade as beams of strong sunlight throw the scene into relief. She's reading a book and whatever it is has her captivated. On the table next to her is a small vase of flowers, a half-drunk glass of orange juice, and our phone. She looks so content, lost in her distraction. Do I really want to disturb this study in solitude? I would paint this moment if I were an artist.

I lean against the bar out of sight and observe her. I recall being in a similar situation a few girlfriends ago. Standing in a pub out of view because I was late, not by much, but I was late. I was reluctant to join my then girlfriend because I knew her reaction would be difficult. Unpleasant. So, I stood where I was, thinking over and over again, this relationship isn't right. This is not how it's supposed to be. And I don't want to live in fear like this. I downed my beer and walked out. I never saw the girl again.

But today when I greet K, she won't mind one little bit if I am late, early, or whatever… she will be simply glad, happy and content to see me. I know it.

I get within a few metres and when she looks up and puts her book down, I see what she's reading – a book on sea kayaking! I chuckle and she looks at me, smiles and says, 'What?'

'Oh, nothing,' I say. 'I have something for you by the way.'

'Ah, what's that?'

I sit down beside her and reach into the deep back pocket of my shorts and pull out a stick of glue.

'Eh, what?'

I lift K's hand.

'This is just to make sure we're never apart again,' I say, and spread the glue generously across her palm and then mine before pressing them firmly together.

K finds it hilarious. It's lovely to watch her uninhibited laughter. Her eyes sparkle with joy and excitement.

'I have something else for you,' I say.

'Handcuffs?'

'No, but it's a thought. It's the letters of the alphabet thrown together to form a poem of sorts.'

'Another one?' K bounces in her seat. 'Will you read it to me now, please?'

'Yes, I think I can because it's quite short. Less chance of any of that public weeping stuff!'

the temerity of infatuation
i need to be with you or i perish (i want you).
i cannot be good, or thoughtful or kind (i want you).
i cannot rest, settle or sit for any one moment (i want you).
i cannot hear the things other people are saying (i want you).
i keep seeing you but it is not you (i want you).
i keep answering the phone, but it is not you (i want you).
i cannot laugh or smile at any one thing (i want you).
i fail to see what i am looking at (i want you).
i cannot remember where i have just been (i want you).
i cannot eat a proper meal (i want you).
i cannot sleep at night (i want you).
you no longer linger on my tee-shirt
(i want you).

K shakes her head from side to side like a metronome. 'That is exactly how it has been for me. That is how it *is* for me.'

'Has resonance, then? Thought it might. It's why I wrote it.'

There is quiet while K reads the poem to herself.

'Can I keep this?' There's an odd look of desperation on her face.

'Of course. It's yours. I wrote it for you alone.'

We sidle closer together and our hips meet to say hello. I grab K's sticky hand again. 'Hey!'

'What?'

'Come here and kiss me.'

'Okay… if I must.'

Friday 6th August

11:00
+19°
Overdraft: To max
Business head on: To max
BS barometer: To max

We're in front of the business angels and Graham is running through the all-important projections for the next five years.

12:40
It's over. Not just the meeting but also their interest in our business.

Bollocks!

12:50
In the pub.

'Well, it was always a bit of a long shot,' says Graham, 'upon reflection.'

I put my head in my hands and thump my forehead with my fists.

'Right, we're going to need a new game plan, then. Something that is going to turn this little business of ours around.'

'Yup, I agree,' says Graham.

'Fancy another drink then?'

'Go on then! Make it a pint. Let's do some serious brainstorming!'

14:55
I've dropped Graham off and with a more positive spirit am heading over to Lois's.

15:05

My Nokia rings. It's K.

Me: 'Hello! You okay?'

K: 'Yes, I am, thank you. How did your meeting go?'

Me: 'Ask a different question, please.'

K: 'Ah! Okay, I will. Are you still coming back on Sunday evening, as I was going to book a table at Scallop Bay restaurant?'

Me: 'Yes, that would be fantastic. Ask if we can have a table by the window, that way we can watch the sunset drop behind Brownsea and the other islands.'

K: 'My thoughts entirely. What sort of time do you think?'

Me: 'I'm hoping to be home by 7pm. I can pick you up if you like. Will you be available then?'

K: 'I think so. I should have an empty house by teatime.'

Me: 'Great.'

K: 'I spent most of this afternoon in the surf shop with Robert and Michael choosing their new boards. They're so excited about going surfing! They took forever to choose. I didn't realise there were so many different types!'

Me: 'I understand completely! When it comes to making very important decisions about boards 'n' boats, these things must not be rushed.'

K: 'Well, we got there in the end but Robert was so particular. Everything has to be exactly to his liking. The man in the shop was very patient with them though. Anyway, that's their two birthday presents done and dusted.'

K: 'Please drive carefully. I know what your driving's like. I need you in one piece.'

Me: 'Will do. But there's nothing wrong with my driving, it's other people's driving. And I—'

Bleep.

Me: 'Phone battery's going…'

K: 'Hello?'

Silence.

TWO
DAYS
LATER

Sunday 8th August

19:10
F1-2 SW +24°
Our first date.

I've just driven past the 'Welcome to Dorset' county sign, which means there's not too far to go. I've texted K to say I'm running fifteen minutes late. It won't take us long to get down to Sandbanks, take the chain ferry across to Studland and then dinner on the beach.

19:25
Outside K's house and there are enough butterflies in my stomach to replace the Lepidoptera collection of the Natural History Museum. Not sure why I'm so nervous. I guess it is a mix of the excitement of seeing K and the worry of parking right outside her house, somewhere I ought not to be.

My nerves get the better of me and I reverse up a little further along the road. I text K and, in the mirror, soon see her jog towards me. God, she looks sexy when she runs! How is that even possible?

I lean over and push open the passenger door – and promptly regret it. I should get out and hold the door open for her. I blame it on my unsettled state and apologise.

'Don't be so silly,' she says. I'm calmed in an instant.

We head down to the ferry and the car is brimming with zestful energy; zing 'n' zang bouncing between us – enough to power the car. There's so much vitality it's almost a fire hazard. K's radiating enough of her special K-energy and I'm almost frightened to touch her. One of our lightning bolts while we're in the car and it could be curtains!

19:45

We're on the chain ferry rumbling our way across to the restaurant. As if on cue the weather has cleared, and it has turned into a perfect summer's evening. The sun is still high in the west and pleasantly warming. There's not a cloud in the grand dome of ultramarine, no sea breeze to speak of, and the unruffled water is a deep, enticing shade of jade. Black-headed gulls dance around our heads, keen for scraps, and a lone tern, with the wings of an angel, performs a majestic, languid dance ahead of us. I wrap my arms around K; we hold our breath and become one as we relish the moment.

K looks at me; her eyes are wide and the thoughts behind them are bursting through. And, if I am honest, there is a new sensuality about her that I've not previously encountered. Her heart is racing so much I can feel the beats pulsing through my fingertips. 'We've not even made it off the ferry yet,' she giggles.

20:00

We're seated next to the long window with a view across the harbour towards the islands.

'This is perfect,' K says, as she settles into her chair.

'The owner has his own fishing boat, the blue-and-white one moored there, and I often see him heading out to sea at dawn. He's either going fishing or over to France to buy fish. It's what makes the food here so memorable.'

K looks radiant tonight. She's wearing an oatmeal linen off-the-shoulder dress, her favourite type it seems, and a light blue cardigan draped over her shoulders. Her sun-streaked chestnut hair hangs loose, and I have a powerful urge to run my fingers through it. No handbag or accessories – that's not her – and she is shod in a smart pair of leather sandals. A different, slightly more elegant pair than the red ones she wears to swimming. She uses no make-up, no mascara or any lipstick; there's clearly no need – or indeed, I sense – any interest in such things.

'I haven't been out to dinner for ages. Tim doesn't really do that sort of thing, at least not just the two of us. Since we had the children there's never been the time. Dinner parties, yes – but actually out to dinner? I can't think of the last time!'

'I think you're part of a grand experiment he's masterminding. He's discovered the secret of eternal youth and you're his star patient. In a way, similar to keeping rhubarb in the dark but in reverse; by not taking you out he's ensuring you are not ageing, nor is there accelerated growth.'

'Are you saying I need to grow?'

'No, I believe he has got his fertiliser mix sorted perfectly! I just think he's missing a marketing opportunity.'

'You could be right. He does bring home some very odd medicines at times.'

'Well, there you are. You're part of an experiment and haven't realised it. Going out to dinner will upset his test results.'

We sip our wine and look out across the harbour. K slips off her sandals and places her bare feet on top of mine. She glances at me coyly, as if to say *I'm just so happy right now, right here in this moment*. I peek a look back at her and try to give her the same message… and it seems to have the right effect as she breaks into her beamy smile; a smile that pushes up to her cheekbones, creating a desirable concave arc that curves around to the edge of her chin – a smile that is kind, open and friendly. The type of smile that, if seen by a crying baby, conveys instant tranquillity, untroubledness, kindness and oodles of warmth.

K turns her head to look out across the bay and I study her profile. At this irredeemable moment, she is the most beautiful woman I have ever laid eyes upon.

'I've been thinking,' I say, 'we should travel further along the Purbeck this week. I know some fantastic places where we could swim off the ledges, have our own private bathing spot. Spend the day down there and more. It's a coastline full of wows.'

K leans towards me. Her eyes are ablaze once again. Hesitantly she whispers, 'Maybe we could camp overnight?'

'That would be fun, and if the weather stays like this, we wouldn't need a tent, just a sleeping bag.'

I realise I've used the singular form, but K doesn't seem to have noticed. One bag, two people. Sounds good to me.

K carries on excitedly chatting about the idea of camping; she starts making lists of the things we might need. I retreat inwardly. On the many long walks along the Purbeck coast I've done since living in Dorset – in the bitterest winter winds and in the skin-burnishing heat of high summer – I've noted a number of places I always imagined would make wonderful overnight spots. I'm not sure why I mentally logged this information, but, whatever the reason, it's proving invaluable now. I decide on a particular location that I know K will adore. High up on a chalk clifftop, dramatic and with unparalleled views across the sea but secluded and as close to nature as it's possible to get.

'I know somewhere,' I suggest. 'Leave it to me. It will be perfect.'

'Tomorrow night then, after swimming?'

'Yes. I'll check the forecast, but tomorrow night it is then.'

We both fall silent, clearly thinking about what we've just committed to. A whole night together. A remote venue. One sleeping bag. We smile apprehensively at one other like two runaways. We've been given two new passports but are not totally sure what to do with them or where to go.

Our food arrives and our conversation retreats to the everyday.

21:15

I suggest we walk down to the beach by the water's edge to watch the sun sink behind the distant Purbeck hills.

We sit on the dry sand and let the tiny lapping waves softly brush our toes. I put my arm around K and as she leans onto my shoulder, we let time and the cares of the world slip away.

'You know,' K says, ever so softly, 'I sense with every beat of our hearts there is something very special going on.'

Darkness has fallen and we have the beach to ourselves. The only illumination comes from the lights across the harbour. A shimmering amber-yellow reflection as the sea gently heaves and subsides.

'Hey!' K says suddenly.

'Yes?'

'Fancy a skinny-dip?'

I'm startled by the suggestion and maybe a little shocked. I look at her and wonder quite how much wine we've drunk.

'You mean go for a skinny-dip now? Right this second?'

'Yes! It will be lovely. The water's warm, there's no one about. C'mon, let's do it!'

'Okay. Why not. For sure! Let's go for it!'

'Yes!'

We jump to our feet quickly. I check the beach to make sure no one's still hanging about and, in those seconds, K has hoisted her dress over her head and is already unclipping her bra. It falls to her feet. She grins at me and then starts laughing as I fumble at my belt.

'C'mon, get a move on!'

I give up trying to undo the belt and yank everything down in one go. Suddenly, unexpectedly, I'm naked.

K, with rather more grace, slips from her knickers and we stand opposite one another. K grabs my hand. 'Let's run in together.'

I nod in agreement.

We turn towards the sea and lunge at the water, sprinting through the shallows, yelping as the water splashes up our legs and bare skin. The shock is exhilarating and as if choreographed, we both flop into the deeper water simultaneously, making one big splash. Woah! The water is much colder out here. We instantly hug each other. K wraps her legs around my hips and her arms around the back of my neck, and clings to me. Her face is so close to mine I can feel her breath on my cheek. It is sublime – and exquisitely, tantalisingly erotic. I place my hand on the back of her head and gently guide it to the side of my neck. I have one arm underneath her bum holding her into me and K is gripping my waist firmly with her thighs. There's a lot of unexpected skin contact, and I feel the warmth from her open legs emanate onto my stomach. I say to myself, *I think this is the most sensual moment I have ever experienced* and then, a moment later, overwrite it. I don't *think*, I *know* this is the most sensual moment I have ever experienced.

I tug K's hair lightly and move my mouth towards hers. Her soft lips meet mine and we kiss passionately while optimising every area of skin contact, pressing ourselves deep into one another. But it's not enough. Skin-to-skin connection is just not enough. I need more. I want more. I feel I want to be beneath her skin. I want to unzip her, unfasten her, undo her and climb inside her. I want to feel and live every jumping, thumping, trembling moment of her heart. Circulate about her fragile female frame like a spring tide overfall on a zephyrless day. I want to connect and share energies; around, about, over, above and – most critically – in.

21:50

We float as if we had fallen overboard. Except we do not wish to be rescued.

Gradually the cool of the water becomes our undoing, literally, and we break apart. We begin to breaststroke our way back towards the beach, giggling. We're both high as kites, buzzing on endorphins and hardly behaving like the sensible forty-year-olds we're supposed to be. But who cares!

'Wouldn't it be funny if someone has stolen our clothes,' I gasp.

'Maybe they've been selective and left behind just an odd item or two for us to share. That could be interesting!'

'We would have to make a run for it. Be the first cross-dressers to streak over on the chain ferry. Let's hope the police aren't about!'

We bound through the shallows to the shore in unison and find our clothes are intact. We throw them on and make a frantic run for the last ferry of the evening.

As we near the ramps of the ferry, K turns to me and says, 'You know, the best thing about tonight is knowing I can see you again tomorrow.'

Amen to that.

Monday 9th August

20:25
SW +23°

Swim training has finished and I'm waiting in the car for K. In the back are a few camping items and the plan is to head to the coast, grab a pub supper, then walk the couple of miles over the downs to our secluded spot on the Jurassic Coast.

The glorious weather seems like it is set to continue through to September, equalling 1976 as the hottest summer on record.

'Sorry. The girls in the changing room wouldn't stop chatting tonight. In the end I told them I had to go!'

'No probs. I'm sure if they knew the reason why, they'd fully understand! I don't think anyone suspects anything, do you?' I ask rhetorically. 'No one has said anything to me, but then, blokes are a bit slow on the uptake in matters such as this.'

'No one has said anything to me directly or indirectly either, but I think one or two of the girls have twigged we *might-like-each-other-a-bit*.'

I'm not sure whether to laugh or log it as a warning.

20:55
We're eating dinner together for the second night in a row. In a pub this time, and the surroundings couldn't be more different. K's eyes say, *Check out those characters at the bar*, so I turn to take a peek. Yes, the pub is properly rustic with authentic locals who speak the old Dorset dialect.

'It's like an episode of *The Archers*,' K says.

'Should I up the accent a bit more? Alreit me daaaarling?'

'No. You have a lovely voice, please don't change it.'

'Alright, but I know a few old Dorset names for things. Here's one I remember – what's a Polly Washdish?'

'No idea.'

'It's old Dorset for a pied wagtail.'

'Hah!'

'What are blue buttons?'

'Nope.'

'Field scabious, the dainty lilac blooms you see on wayside banks.'

'I like that.'

'What is a dumbledoor?'

'I think I know this one. A bumblebee!'

'Correct. I love the old delightful-sounding vernacular.'

'Maybe we should go and ask those two old chaps sitting at the bar. I bet they know a few,' K suggests.

'I'm sure they would.'

22:00

'I suppose we should make a move and get to our bedroom before room service knocks off for the night,' I say.

'Yes. I'm eager to see the view through the bedroom window.'

We grab our things from the car and start walking up the long-sloped track through the chalk downlands. As we lose the light from the small village, the stars begin to make themselves known and, as we walk further towards the coast, are properly unveiled. We stop and look up in wonder at the grandeur of the Milky Way, the edge-on spectacle of our galaxy – a sight that has stunned modern humans since they first turned their eyes heavenward. As our eyes adjust, we can pick out Polaris and the constellations of the Plough and the 'W' of Cassiopeia and then grumble at our ignorance.

'To think,' I say, 'less than one hundred years ago man navigated his way around the globe by the stars and now you and I are struggling to identify more than a couple of constellations.'

K's hand is in mine as we progress up the chalky track. We swap sides a few times, experimenting. Sometimes K tries walking on my right and then on my left but, for some inexplicable reason, when she's on my left holding my left hand I feel so *entirely complete* that when her hand is withdrawn from mine, I find it deeply unsettling. However, when she walks on my right, again with her hand thrust in mine, the feeling is – relatively ordinary.

My mother used to keep two tiny model jeeps in her desk drawer, a green one and a red one. Inside each was a magnet and as a child, I would play with them on the tiled kitchen floor. As I moved the front of one jeep closer and closer to the rear of the other, they would, at a critical distance, suddenly leap across the remaining inches to crash into each other. However, if I placed the two jeeps face to face and moved one towards the other, again, at a critical distance, one would retreat. Repelled. In much the same way, K's and my hands have polarity. I have no idea why this should be so, but it's further evidence that we are like finely machined parts, destined to fit together in one particular way and with tolerances measured on the nanoscale.

As we crest the first hill and start on a short downhill section, I bend to tie my shoelace. Stooped, I witness a tiny shimmering fluorescent green light. 'Look, look. A glow worm!'

We squat down to take a closer look.

'They're everywhere! Look! Look, over there,' she exclaims.

We stand up and amongst the short grass and hummocks, and as far as our eyes can see, there are thousands of tiny natural green-hued lanterns, luminescent, magically carpeting our world and illuminating our onward path.

'I've not seen them since I was a little girl,' K says, 'but never as many as this. It's almost as if they are here just for us. Showing us the way to our bedroom above the sea.'

The salt-laden sea air hits us as we reach the last half mile of our walk. In daylight, the view is breath-taking; at night, under the stars and in the light of a waning moon, the view is austere, profound, ancient, compulsive and as indifferent as majesty. The sea from up here looks as flat as a tray of quicksilver, and shimmies enticingly. We near the top of the cliff, where we can hear a muted thud followed by a sharp crackle as a wave meets the bottom of the cliff and grating pebbles on the narrow beach roll back towards the sea.

'I am in awe. Where are we?' K asks in a whisper.

'If I tell you, I might have to kill you. Seriously, you must promise not to tell anyone. We're on White Nothe and down there,' I point to the west, 'is one of my most favourite places ever – Ringstead Bay.'

'Oh, my.'

'If we make it through the night, we can wander down to the café for brekky in the morning. Now, if Madam would like to follow me, I'll show you to your room. This way, please.'

I take K's hand and lead her down the steep, narrow cliff face. It's a long, winding descent, but the footing is solid and with no wind to buffer us about, the traverse around the front of the cliff is relatively risk-free tonight.

'How are you with heights?' I ask K.

'Sort of okay, but it's just as well it's bloody dark, that's all I'm saying,' she replies anxiously. 'Looks like I'll have to put my trust in you!'

'What a foolish woman you are.'

As we round the corner of the cliff, a chalky outcrop comes into view. It is flat, sheltered, and rich with thick green hill-grass several inches deep. Comfortable to lie upon and a perfect place to spend the night.

'And here we are,' I say proudly. 'Our billet. But please don't roll about too much in the night otherwise you might find yourself – er – in the sea.'

'What! You are kidding, aren't you?'

'It's fine. Let me show you.'

I take K's arm and guide her to the edge. We peer over.

'What a miraculous view. And yes, I see what you mean. As long as I don't sleepwalk, I think I should be fine!'

'Please, don't do that. I will be holding on to you though.' I reassure her.

K turns from the edge, slips her hands beneath my arms and slots herself into me.

'This is so much nicer than I imagined,' she says. 'It's going to be an amazing night.'

I unroll the sleeping mats and place them side by side. I unfurl the sleeping bag and place the feet end nearest the cliff edge. K pulls out two puffy pillows from her bag and puts them near the cliff face.

'Time for ablutions and then to bed?' I say, with a certain forced levity.

'Yes, but no bedtime story?'

'Let's see, shall we? Perhaps, if you're really good.'

It's obvious we're both nervous.

I hunker down and test the foam for comfort. There are a few bumps and I shuffle things around trying to make the two mats meet properly in the middle. I crawl inside the sleeping bag and look up at the stars. Woah! I feel something shift within my psyche. It's a physical response to an age-old wonder. I am suitably grateful to the gods for the knowledge that K will adore our bedroom view when she returns.

The sleeping bag feels plenty warm enough, but I've brought along a thin wool blanket in case it should turn unexpectedly cold during the night. We are in England after all. That said, I'm banking on two warm bodies, cocooned for the duration, providing adequate mutual warmth.

K is back, wearing a short-sleeved tee-shirt that goes almost to her knees. I try, really try, but can't help myself. *I wonder if she has anything on under that tee-shirt.*

I unthinkingly change in front of her. I grab my top and slip it over my head. I begin to pull down my shorts – then something makes me stop. I mean, what exactly *is* the correct etiquette here? Strip completely and be regarded as *pushing it a bit*, or keep my shorts on and locate myself in the *a-bit-of-a-prude* camp?

I end up indecisively hopping about on one leg, half in, half out, trying to give myself more time to think. All of this would be so much easier if I knew what she was wearing under her tee-shirt! Maybe I could ask? No. I must make the decision myself and make it pretty damn quickly. Pushy? Prudish? Which is it to be? Hang on, I'm a man and she's a woman and we're alone on a cliff top. Surely, it's obvious; it's what every man and woman do, isn't it? BUT – I care for this woman, deeply. I revere this woman with all my being. She is altering my life by the minute. To leap under the covers with everything hanging out would be – disrespectful.

I care, therefore I wear.

Good things come to those who wait, don't they?

I lie on my side next to K with my face in the nape of her neck. I can sense how enthralled she is by the firmament. I turn onto my back and gaze up too. The stars are even brighter now – and there are so many of them. One hundred billion in our galaxy alone, and most of them seem to have put on their finery for our benefit tonight. With no light pollution, each twinkling point is discernible and more colourful than I've ever seen before. They're determined to make themselves individually known to us, saying, *Here I am. I may look small but I can see you, even though you can't always see me.*

It's so quiet, with only the gentle intermittent *thwump* of waves hitting the bottom of the cliff. Everything is still, as if the world, the Universe, has decided to pause from its otherwise urgent progress. Holding its breath in a generously gifted timeout. But our senses are fully awake. How could they not be? The wind-borne aroma of the sea is stronger now, enticing and, in its ancient life-spawning character, more erotic than ever. The refreshing cologne of fresh windswept hill-grass, pungent in the cool night air, offers an almost spiritual counter note.

And then there is K! If nature's fragrances are already enough to satisfy, now I must contend with the aroma of a goddess. Her body, skin, hair gently let seep an intoxicating, bewitching scent. It arouses – and insufflates – at the same time. I worship at the altar of her sensual bodily presence.

As the night wears on, the temperature drops and we turn into each other for warmth. We stare at one another. I kiss her, a slow kiss, a kiss that says there is no need to rush, tonight we have *all the time in the world.* Gradually the movement of lips and tongues slows; instead we seal our lips and breathe into each other. I expel my breath into her slowly, unforced. Instinctively, K does the same. It's as if we're sharing a form of nourishment: the nutrients of life, a source of energy upon which we can gorge all night, filling one another with a rejuvenating life force, each breath as if it is a gift from God.

Tuesday 10th August

04:45
Warm dawn

I'm awake. I feel like I've died and been reborn, so deep has been my sleep, but I dare not move. K is still asleep wrapped around me with her face buried into my neck.

I have a mouth full of chestnut-brown hair; clearly, I've been trying to consume her all night. Our shirts are pushed up and there is much heat and a stickiness from sweat that makes me think our skin has been sealed together as one overnight. *We are going to have to peel ourselves apart,* I say to myself. *It could be very painful.*

I lie still and listen. It's not yet light but dawn can't be far off. The new day's waves thump lazily with a muffled voice into the cliff face down below and I can hear gulls calling, squabbling and getting ready for their busy day ahead. In the distance I can hear the rhythmical *thump-thump* of a diesel-driven fishing boat working the lobster pots somewhere below the lower cliff. I'm in no rush to move and grateful to be here, listening to the world waking, accompanied by K's gentle susurration. Soon I drift back into dreamless sleep.

07:20

I'm awake again and know instantly something is wrong. I sit bolt upright. Where is she? Has she gone? I see K standing further along the cliff top looking out to sea, and my mind flashes to that scene in *The French Lieutenant's Woman.*

She turns and sees me staring at her.

She is soon back under the cover and we cling together once more. It's as if we need to urgently refuel once again.

Time passes and I open my eyes to see K's are already upon me.

'How long have you been watching me?' I ask.

'Oh, a while…'

Then the almost unbearably harsh noise of a helicopter intrudes overhead.

'Sorry,' I say. 'I'm just wondering if that was the rescue helicopter. We're not really supposed to be here.'

'It feels like breakfast time anyway – shall we pack up our stuff?'

'I suppose we should. Actually, I'm really quite hungry.'

'I'm hungry too. A good bacon 'n' egg butty wouldn't go amiss.'

The walk to Ringstead, mostly downhill, takes us past a handful of coastal cottages, St Catherine's Chapel-by-the-Sea and into the hamlet itself.

The café is opening just as we arrive, and we're greeted by the delightful smell of frying bacon and fresh coffee.

We perch ourselves on an outside bench in the already-hot sun and wait impatiently for our food. I'm thinking one butty is not going to be sufficient, so go back to the kiosk and order two more rounds – just in case. K has gone quiet, which makes me think she's on her reserve tank and in desperate need of sustenance.

The food arrives, but, as I anticipated, it's not going to be enough. We dive in like ravenous explorers who have been lost, but who have at last found their way back to camp. Do the fools not know we have trekked miles over hills, spent a night without cover, dodged enemy aviators, to arrive almost on the point of death? Suddenly, the second round of butties turns up. This time there's an extra sausage each and a generous scoopful of beans. I give the cook, who can be seen through the open kitchen door, a big thumbs-up. He nods seriously. Clearly, he had recognised how perilous our situation was.

09:10

I wander over to the far corner of the café, looking at my phone and hoping to get a signal so I can at least send Graham a text. I wander up the road to gain some altitude and finally one measly bar appears.

<Out of signal today, pls email anything urgent. Thanks>

I feel guilty. The business needs my attention and here I am spending my time on the coast. Then I remember it's August. Nothing much happens this month. I feel better and walk back to K with a spring in my step.

'Looks like it's going to be hot. Do you fancy going somewhere very secret?'

'Yes! I'd love that.'

'We'll have to go back to the car first and then head towards Dancing Ledge and to a place I know that's truly special.'

I take a notepad and pen from my bag and quickly sketch an outline of the coast. I mark our current location with an 'x', another where the car is parked, and finally where we need to get to today. K takes the pen from my hand and in turn marks, slowly and suggestively, a much bigger 'X' where we stayed last night.

'A big X means big kisses,' she says, laughing.

'In that case, I need to do something about this small x here. Where we are now.'

I stand up, lean over the table, and kiss her.

After we've sat down again, I remember there's something I've been meaning to ask her.

'You know, I have no idea what it is you actually do for a job.'

K thinks for a moment and a baffled expression settles on her face.

'Come to think of it, I have no idea what it is you do for a job either.'

I wonder if this is unusual. Bothering to find out what the other person does for work after more than eight weeks. Maybe it's the hallmark of the quotidian irrelevance of our daily lives in the face of our exceptional desire to be connected?

K gazes into space for a moment then says, 'If you think about it, when it comes to the affairs of the heart these things *should* be irrelevant.'

'Absolutely, I concur.'

10:55

We set off along the beach – my favourite beach – and discover that K has never been here before. Tim takes them further west to Devon and Cornwall but never to this part of Dorset. Now K is wondering why, too.

'I think it might be a work thing, in that he wants to get out of Dorset when on holiday. As a child, he spent a lot of time on the north coast of Cornwall. It *is* beautiful, but it's not the same as here.'

'Have you heard how they are getting on?' I ask.

'Not yet, but Tim said he'd phone in the evenings, so that's why I should be at home tonight.'

I glance at K and there is evident anxiety in her eyes.

I quickly change the subject.

13:30

We clamber down to my secret bathing ledges. The breeze is blowing briskly from the west, right into where I'm planning to get to, pushing the waves onto the ledges. They are a spectacular sight as they break in a column of spume before retreating shamefaced as if to say, *Don't mind us, we're just doing what waves must do.*

'We might get a bit wet,' I shout to K, who's right behind me.

'Bloody hell. Are we going down there?' She points to the big rocky outcrops below the cliff face and our destination.

'Yes. It'll be fine. You'll be fine. Follow me.'

We clamber down. Although the tide is still coming in, there are large areas of the ledges that are bone dry and out of the wind.

'How do you know all these places?'

'Years of exploring this section of coastline. I've been waiting what feels like a lifetime to show them to the right person.'

We reach a ledge where the breeze is mitigated. The surface is hard but flat, though some regions are heavily pitted and walking on them, particularly in flip-flops, is painful. The sea is only a few metres away and the most energetic waves can reach our platform, but the majority break below us.

15:45

'You know we've got the Brownsea sea swim on Sunday? It's four and a half miles and we really ought to train for it.'

'I was worried before, but now I'm seriously concerned about completing the distance. There's swim training Thursday night, isn't there? I'm banking on that being enough!'

'Yes. Yes, there is, but I was thinking – perhaps we should go for a sea swim now?'

'What? It looks really rough. We could hurt ourselves on those rocks, and it's deep water that will be freezing. It's nothing like the shallower and safer harbour!'

'It'll be fine. Look down there.' I point to a small inlet where, a hundred years ago, barges would come in to pick up quarried limestone.

I take K's hand and guide her down to the bottom section of the ledge.

'It's quite slippery here, so be careful.'

'Oh, I see what you mean. It doesn't look so bad, does it? Still, look at the waves, they could easily push us onto those big rocks.'

'You have to time it so that you surf in on a wave that forces you up this gulley. Then you can tell your boys you've been out surfing!'

K is far from convinced.

'Well, I can't go in on my own. You must come in with me. That's the deal,' I say.

'So both of us get washed out to sea!'

'It'll be fine. Come on. Where's all the bravery gone from the other night? Best to keep *some* clothes on though this time. Just in case the coastguard is called out to rescue us!'

'Okay then. But I'm staying close to you.'

We pick our way back up the rocks and dig around for our swim kit.

I casually strip and stand completely naked in front of K. She looks at me and pulls down her beach shorts followed quickly by her knickers, and for the second time in forty-eight hours we are stood naked opposite one another, although in full daylight this time. We don't say anything; both of us a little surprised, I think. K bends down and picks out her swim costume and wiggles into it. I step into my swim jammers and pull them up snugly. *It's just so bloody easy with this woman.*

I take K's hand again and we tiptoe our way down the rocks to stand opposite the gulley. The waves are crashing around our knees and the spray is flicking up into our faces. Yes, the water here is pretty cold.

'We're going to have to time this right. Jump in together when the wave is above our knees and is about to fall back. Okay?'

'Okay, but I'm hanging onto you!'

'Ready? Three… two… one. Go!'

We both leap at the same time as the wave is sucked back out to sea. Immediately, we are carried eight or nine metres away from the ledge on an exhilarating ride. The water is really cold!

'Shit! That's chilly,' I shout.

K is treading water madly. Her eyes are wide open – like Bambi who has just sat down on something very sharp. I begin to get the giggles. This is so insane.

'Bloody hell, we need to keep moving or we're going to freeze.'

I swim over to K and grab hold as another wave lifts us up and makes us feel very mortal. I slide my legs around her hips and pull her into me, but it's too rough to be passionate out here.

'It's too cold to swim. I need my wetsuit for this,' K splutters.

'It's the deep water here – so much colder, isn't it?'

'Let's get out!'

'That's the training all done for Brownsea then.'

We breaststroke quickly back towards the gulley – then hold off a number of metres away so we can time our approach. The waves are really powerful, far too keen to push us in, so we swim on our backs and head back out to sea again. I ponder the best tactic for a few seconds and then say that because of the narrowness of the gulley, we should go in one behind the other.

'I'll lead in and you hang onto my waist,' I shout. 'We'll go in on the next surging wave.'

K merely nods.

'Here's one coming now. Ready? Here we go. Yee-haw!'

K hangs onto my hips as if her life depends on it. Which, in truth, it might. I use my outstretched arms to direct us in and up the gulley. We're moving fast. I grapple for a handhold, knowing I'm only going to have one or two attempts at it before we get pulled back out again – but by then we'll be well and truly out of control. K's trying to get some purchase with her feet, but the gulley floor has been worn smooth over the aeons and is far too slippery. I can feel her scrabbling about. I make one more lunge at a small crevice and, fortuitously, manage to get my fingers behind the lip. It's enough to allow me to pull us both upright before the wave retreats. I lift K up out of the gulley and we quickly climb to higher ground.

'Where are the towels?' K asks shivering.

'Err, excuse me, but bloody hell…'

It's the first time I've really heard her swear.

'Well, that was really exhilarating, quite wild!'

'I told you it would be fine. Didn't I?' I say with a grin across my face.

K pulls the towel assertively from my hand and chunders an expletive.

We move to a corner of the ledge that's a sun trap, trying to warm and dry our bodies. I stand behind K and wrap myself around her calmingly, running my hands up and down her body to get the blood circulating and she soon warms up.

There's not a soul about. The occasional boat can be seen battling its way through the waves, but they're at least a mile or more out to sea. Behind us, one hundred feet above or so, is the cliff top and coastal path. Apart from a couple of seagulls languidly riding the updraft off the rock face, we could be virtually the last people on earth. If we had got into serious trouble in the sea – and, to be honest, we were not too far short of that – well, no one was coming to our aid anytime soon. Death in liquid love…

17:15

I come to. K is sitting with her back against the cliff wall reading. I am surprised to find my head is in her lap. She looks down to me.

'Hello, sleepyhead.'

Her voice is something I am now addicted to.

'Have I been asleep long?'

K leans down and kisses me on my forehead.

'Yes. Hours.'

I stay where I am and shut my eyes but can't resist the temptation to open one to spy on her. She's reading a paperback – Edith Wharton's *The Age of Innocence*. I always get the feeling Newland Archer wants, more than anything, to break out of the stuffy, restrictive high society setting Wharton has placed him in, and the free-spirited countess could really make him happy. But it's all too inevitable, tragic really, when in the end Archer sticks with May Welland out of convention and fear of the uncertain.

I want to tell K something important. It's the way I have been feeling since we first connected on the water in the kayaks. It has become an overwhelming thing. The three most important words anyone can say to another. Three words that more or less ensure the continuation of our species, no less. Words I have only uttered once before, naively (if I'm truthful). And this time, I can say them with far greater insight about their meaning – undoubtedly so – with certainty and sincerity, for this little woman has got me – and oh-so easily.

I love you.

As I look up at K, I can think only of this: speak those three words.

Tell her you love her. Tell her because you do love her. Of course, the angels Raqib and Atid are sat on my shoulders and he that is on my left whispers, 'You have only known her for a few weeks, how can you possibly *love* her?'

So, I remain silent. Perplexed and somewhat frustrated.

K puts down her book and kisses me again – this time on the lips.

'You know, it's getting quite late, I think we should be heading back,' she says.

For now, the more garrulous angel is in the ascendant.

But I will tell her. And soon. *I have to.*

Wednesday 11th August

09:15
Still breezy F5-6, SW, +24°
K forecast: ↑ ↑
Office forecast: ↑
Exercise outlook: ↑

The fuse is burning…

There is a lot to catch up on today. But first, I must call Lois. There have been several missed calls from her on my Nokia. Awkward.

13:10
I've managed to forestall any serious investigation into my recent whereabouts by Lois. She's frantically busy with work, so that helps, but I feel sick at this deception.

K is working today but finishes at 3pm. It is possible she can come over to my house tonight – for the first time. But I'm trying not to get too excited…

15:15
Text from K.

> *<You OK for later? Can come over. All fine here>*

> *<Yes. Come over. Will cook for you>*

Now, there's poetic licence in my using the word 'cook'. Yes, I can cook, sort of. But my repertoire extends to three varieties of much the same thing – all rice-based. As this is K's first visit to my house, I'll have two subsequent opportunities to impress, culinarily speaking, before my cover is blown and I am shown to be nothing more than a cooking fraud.

18:00

Trying to remain calm but am pacing around the house. I can't believe the woman I've dreamt of every night since I first saw her in the pool in late May is going to be here, within these four walls. Maybe it's all a bizarre test? We've been given this interlude by the gods to prove, once and for all, what hopeless dreamers K and I are… and have been from the beginning.

18:15

K should be here soon. I'm thumbing through my CD collection, trying to decide what sort of music to play when she arrives. Bowie? Possible. The Boss? Depends which album. Paul Weller? The Stones? Probably not. Van Morrison? Yes. I flick open the case of 'Best of' and hit Play. Hope she'll be impressed.

I open up the French windows and lay the garden table. The sun is streaming onto the terrace. Tonight, the view from the garden has got the message and is playing along for all it's worth. I wonder what K will think of my little cottage beneath the big green hill.

I can hear a car drawing up.

18:20

She opens the side gate and walks along the side of the house, not stopping at the open kitchen door. She continues into the garden, up the steps and across the lawn to the bottom of the garden. A woman on a mission.

And I understand exactly why.

When I first saw the cottage a number of summers ago, it had been empty for some time. It was by chance that I was driving past. I had stopped, reversed and taken a quick look at the place. Thank heavens I did! I had opened the dilapidated side gate, walked down the side of the house and straight to the end of the garden where I stood, transfixed, by the hill. Fascinated by its sheer size, shape and verdancy. Interest in the cottage itself was secondary. Only sometime later did I bother to inspect the interior.

K has just done the same thing.

'Wine?' I shout from the kitchen window.

'Your view is incredible. I can understand why you live here.'

I pour K her drink, but she seems not yet ready to settle.

'Would you like to see the rest of the cottage, then?' I ask.

'Yes, yes, please.'

We go inside.

K hears the music. 'I've got this CD,' she says with a smile, as we pass through the living room.

As we wander in and out of the very modest-sized rooms, K doesn't say a great deal but her shining eyes tell me she approves.

'It's *exactly* how I imagined it would be,' she says, shaking her head. 'How amazing is that! It is absolutely perfect.'

'Perfect in the summer perhaps, but not so much in the winter! It can be damn cold when that westerly wind blows over the hill!'

We wander downstairs and into the kitchen, and I turn on the heat on the cooker and begin to get the food underway.

'I've brought some fresh salad with me. I'm guessing you don't eat enough greens,' she declares.

'How dare you! I eat loads of leaves and those green types of things. Always munching on them. Non-stop. Morning, noon and night. Never without a leaf in my hand.'

I return to conjuring up my exotic rice dish perfected after years of practice.

K comes back with a large filled salad bowl.

'I have a box delivered every week from the local organic farm shop, so there's always lots of fresh veg and greens. To be honest, I struggle to use it all sometimes.'

'Great. Well, send any surplus my way then, please.'

'I will. You clearly need it!'

19:45

We're sitting at the garden table.

'If it proves inedible, we can always nip down the pub.'

'Don't be mad, it looks delicious.' K puts a forkful of risotto into her mouth. 'It's really good.'

K eats slowly before reaching for the water jug. My intuition tells me she has something she needs to say. Something important.

'You're so kind to me. Really, so kind. I'm not used to any of this.'

'What do you mean? This is nothing—'

K interrupts me before I can finish. 'No, not this, the food. This. Us. *You and me*. The way you are with me. I've never… never felt like this before.'

I put my arm around her and squeeze her into me. 'It is new for me, too,' I whisper. 'This depth. I am in uncharted waters also.'

K suddenly drops her fork onto the plate with a crash that startles me. Before I know what's happening, she throws her arms around my neck, gripping me so tightly I can't breathe. She is crying. Tears unleashed from the very depths of her soul.

I rock her gently while kissing the top of her head as you might comfort a child. She is wracked with sobs, burying herself into me. My own tamped-down restraint gives way and eight weeks of confusion, heightened emotion and quickened-living claws its way to the surface. I bite down hard on my lip, but it is hopeless. I too weep – wildly, exaggeratedly, ridiculously.

'I didn't mean to make you cry.' I am apologising but have no idea why.

'It has overcome me. I am so frightened by the immensity of it.'

'*Except I be by Sylvia in the night, There is no music in the nightingale; Unless I look on Sylvia in the day, There is no day for me to look upon*. And therein lies our problem, I believe.'

'How apt Shakespeare always is. When at university, I regularly used to go to the RSC. Still do, when I think of it,' K says still sobbing.

'Perhaps we can go together?' I suggest.

'Yes, let's. My parents don't live too far away from there—'

K stops herself, realising the significance of what she was on the point of saying.

I smile. 'Too much, yes, too soon.'

'Yes. Too much, too soon.'

21:50

'So, you're not working tomorrow but you will be on Friday morning, and Tim is back Friday afternoon?'

'Yes.'

'So, you can stay tonight and tomorrow night?'

'Yes.'

Before I realise what's happening, K jumps on me, pinning me to the floor. I put up pitiful resistance.

'Two whole nights… if that's okay with you!' she says, her face in mine.

'I should probably consult my diary.'

'You do that, Mister. In the meantime, I'm not moving from here.'

I put my arm around K's midriff and spin her onto her back in one fluid movement. I kneel above her, my arms either side of her head and look carefully into her eyes. The sun has set, the music has stopped, and the only sound is coming through the open French windows as my friendly blackbird insistently chirps at something presumably less friendly.

I stare avidly into K's eyes and she responds, fixing her gaze directly up at me. But it's too far away. Any distance apart is too far away. I drop lower and rest my mouth on her lips, locking my eyes into hers so we are no more than an eyelash apart. We stare intently into one another, not blinking, just staring… and a new world begins to open up, as if we've just triggered the special password to allow us into a new astral dimension. We step through easily and into a place that is so full of colour and richness that I don't believe there is a word yet created to singularly describe the intensity of hues that exist.

Colours that are so saturated with vibrancy that they almost feel solid to the touch, yet they are constantly moving; these swirling, twisting, forming, ever-evolving clouds of iridescent light are like friendly storm clouds gathering – unstill, perpetually evolving and consolidated in their form. It is a momentous kaleidoscope of unworldly colour, vivid and intense, a dimension where no artist could ever capture the moment on canvas nor even match the movement of the colours – nor the depth of the evolving hues. It is a special place to be, this window to the interior of the soul.

22:45

I lift K from the sitting room floor and carry her up and around the steep flight of stairs to my bedroom. I place her gently on the white duvet-covered bed. The room is suffused with silver moonlight and I rest my head on her chest. Her breath is coming in hurried pants. I kneel and pull off my tee-shirt and K helps me tug it over my head. She spreads her palms and places them on my chest.

'Your heart is pounding,' she says softly. I place my hand on top of hers and press down. She can feel the strength of each beat.

'I want to get next to your skin,' I say urgently.

I reach for the hem of K's cotton top and she lifts herself off the bed to allow me to pull it over her head. It slips off easily and she lets herself drop back to the duvet and onto my right hand that unclasps her bra. I slide my hand around to her soft front and sweep it to one side. I press myself down onto K and feel her extraordinary femininity. I seek out her hands and we interlock our fingers, instinctively squeezing palm-to-palm, letting our energies comingle.

'We still have too many clothes on.'

We both roll onto our sides and remove the remaining items. K brings her knees up to her chest as I slide a black pair of cotton-lace knickers along her thighs and over her feet. I have a cheeky thought. *Are these the same black pair of knickers that I've had in my possession before?*

'Here we are naked yet again,' K says seductively. 'Tis becoming something of a habit!' We lie skin-to-skin and feel so alive, like I have been secretly wired into the mainframe of the Southern Electricity board; there's so much activity flowing but all I feel I need to do right now is lie motionless and engage the moment and ponder. *Why has it not felt like this before?*

23:58

It's nearly midnight, we're under the covers, exploring. The chances of getting much slumber are minimal.

'I don't want to miss one minute asleep,' K says. 'I want to witness all this – awake!' K is absolute.

But… I don't know if I have it in me… *not* to step over that borderline.

Argh! And argh again!

Thursday 12th August

09:25
Sunshine everywhere!

It's after nine o'clock and I ought to be at my desk but we're still in the bath and it's not good news: MTB 102 does not run properly when confronted by a sea of bubbles. Its engines are just not powerful enough! K insisted on huge dollops of matcha tea and coconut water bubble bath (Lois's). I'm sulking at the tap-end while K lords it up at the posh-end.

'Perhaps we can take the kayaks out today, go for a paddle. What do you think?' K asks, by way of a peace offering.

'We could,' I say, perking up. 'I've got a wooden two-man boat from the 1950s. He's not been out on the water for ages. Great boat, a bit heavy but perfect for the sea.'

'Oh yes, let's!'

'What about swim training tonight? It's the big race on Sunday. Do you think you can manage both in one day?'

'I'll try. Let's give it a go!'

'Okay, great, sorted. A day out in the kayak, then swimming. Ideal training. We'll be completely stuffed tonight!'

I reach for the soap on a rope and grab the scratchy flannel.

'Turn around and I'll scrub your back.'

10:45
The two-man boat is loaded, my phone is on divert and all guilty feelings about Lois are boxed and sealed with tape. K is by my side

in the passenger seat and, in this moment, I care for nothing else. I'm with the woman who has changed my life and it feels so damn good.

21:15
Back home

We've scoffed a takeaway pizza. It was either that or more of my limited rice-based cooking. A full day in the kayak and by the river, then straight on to swim training, meant we were both in the red zone – with our collective low-fuel light burning brightly.

K pours me a glass of wine; I lie back on the sofa, she cuddles into me, and I hit the remote.

Ten minutes later we're both falling fast asleep.

Friday 13th August

07:00

I wake to the most mesmerising eyes I have ever seen – since last night.

But in them resides deep sorrow. This is our 'last' morning together. After this, who knows when or how we will be able to meet. We will, of course, but it will not be as easy nor as unrestrained and uninhibited as this past week.

Years ago, on the island of Ibiza, I came across a weather-beaten old man sat on a stool at his market stall. He was making and selling highly intricate small wooden boxes. One in particular caught my eye; it had smooth sides, beautifully rounded corners and a lovely feel to the touch. It was about three inches long and an inch wide with a sliding lid that sealed the box tightly. I liked that aspect of it because whatever was placed inside was never going to fall out or be lost easily. I was happy to give the old chap his 150 pesetas and wandered off delighted with my find.

The little box has remained in my desk drawer ever since and, while girlfriends have come and gone, none, not even Lois, have to my mind been 'deserving' enough to warrant being given this cute wooden box with a nice sliding lid and a hand-written message inside. And thank heaven for that! Because now *is* the time.

I suddenly jump out of bed.

K looks at me, startled. 'Is everything okay?'

'Yes, just got to do something – urgently!'

I run into my office, open the desk drawer, and quickly locate the wooden box. I grab a piece of paper and write: *When you open this box, think only of me, for I am with you.* Underneath, I write: *You are the most beautiful woman in the world*. I roll the paper up tightly and place it inside the box, and slide the lid shut.

'Close your eyes,' I say, as I leap back under the covers.

She does.

I lift her hand and place the box into it.

'This is for you. You must keep it with you always. Keep it in a safe place. It's very special. Okay?'

'Yes.'

'You can open your eyes now.'

'Wow! It's lovely. It feels so smooth. What's inside?'

'Open it and see.'

K slowly slides back the lid and carefully takes out the tightly rolled piece of white paper. She begins to read the words aloud.

'When you open this box, think only of me, for I—'

K can't continue but instead throws herself at me. She wraps her arms tightly around my back, squeezing the air out of me.

She is crying.

'I love what you do to me. I'm never going to leave your side. Never.'

Saturday 14th August

09:40
Blue + the sun still shines +24°
Athens Olympics start today!

The postman has just been and asked me to sign for a Recorded Delivery letter. The handwriting on the envelope has doubled my pulse rate. It's from K.

Friday afternoon (and rushing to catch the post!)

'What is past, is prologue'
(E. E. Cummings)

The week that was perfect.

The time is now right to share with you my poem. It has been with me since I first read it as a teenager during my English classes. I was inspired by E. E. Cummings's words and have always believed love like this is out there somewhere. And can be experienced. This past week with you has finally realised that hope and belief.

somewhere I have never travelled, gladly beyond
any experience, your eyes have their silence;
in your most frail gesture are things which enclose me,
or which I cannot touch because they are too near

your slightest look easily will unclose me
though I have closed myself as fingers,
you open always petal by petal myself as Spring opens
(touching skilfully, mysteriously) her first rose

or if your wish be to close me, I and
my life will shut very beautifully, suddenly,
as when the heart of this flower imagines
the snow carefully everywhere descending;

nothing which we are to perceive in this world equals
the power of your intense fragility; whose texture
compels me with the colour of its countries,
rendering death and forever with each breathing

(i do not know what it is about you that closes
and opens; only something in me understands
the voice of your eyes is deeper than all roses)
nobody, not even the rain, has such small hands

and now I have been to that place.

'A pain intensified by the imagination
and prolonged by a hundred echoes'
(Milan Kundera)

and now I have felt that pain.

And we will talk, until thought's melody
Become too sweet for utterance, and it die
In words, to live again in looks, which dart
With thrilling tone into the voiceless heart,
Harmonising silence, without a sound
Our breath shall intermix, our bosoms bound,
And our veins beat together.
(Shelley)

Whenever I am with you, it is so.
And as we and Paulo Coelho know:

'Anyone capable of feeling knows that it is possible to experience pleasure even before touching the other person. The words, the look, all contain the secret of the dance. Anyone who discovers the person they have always dreamt of, knows that sexual energy comes into play before sex even takes place. The greatest pleasure isn't sex but the passion with which it is practised. When the passion is intense, then sex joins in to complete the dance, but it is never the principal aim. Anyone who is in love is making love the whole time even when they're not. When two bodies meet, it is just the cup overflowing.'

Oh, how I wish our cup could overflow!!

However, there are some things I haven't told you. When you and I hold a certain look for the longest time, I imagine you are inside me, moving very slowly with a tenderness I already know. It feels as if it's the first time we have made love in our whole lives. And I know that when you enter me and take me finally to heaven, I will never want to return to earth and to what I have known, but stay forever 'imparadis'd in paradise' (Milton).

Further than this, I cannot see from here. I will have even further to fall if descent inevitably follows the climb, but from that moment out on the water in the kayak when I realised my life had changed, I haven't been able to hold back the tide of emotion that pours copiously from my soul. I am weaker now and incredibly fragile. I hurt easily, am frightened as well as excited by possibility, and carry the heavy burden of shame and guilt each and every day. But try to take you from me – I would cling as a limpet to rock. You are my rock.

This week you have taken me to heaven and I do not want to return to earth and to the life I know...

PS. Why have you kept all others out but allowed me in (as soon as I knocked?)

11:30

I have so much energy, I feel I can climb any mountain and leap from one peak to another all day long. I'm on such a high.

Maybe I can funnel all this energy into the race tomorrow? I'd so love to do well in it.

Sunday 15th August

05:30
Light SW F2-3 +23°
Race day: Brownsea Swim.

It's an early start. Didn't sleep brilliantly it has to be said; too many tactical options swirling around my brain at 3am. My head is fuzzy, and I'm tempted to have a coffee but must resist. Caffeine and swimming do not make a good mix; I cannot afford to cramp up today. Herbal tea it is!

05:45

<Meet u at sign-on?>

05:47

<See you there>

K's children want to watch their mum do the swim, but I had to text her last night and explain that there are no spectators allowed on Brownsea Island. It really is 'competitors only'. As it happens, there's a pro surfing competition on in Bournemouth this weekend, so Tim is taking the children along to watch that instead and K will join them afterwards.

07:20

K has been quite apprehensive in the lead up to the race. Although a really excellent pool swimmer, and a top county level swimmer in her teens, sea swimming is new to her. And it *is* different from pool swimming. There are all sorts of things to contend with, one of which is today's not inconsiderable distance of four and a half miles. The furthest K has ever swum was the pier-to-pier race last month, which was just over a mile. Although she likes to claim she's 'not that competitive', deep down, she still is. Put her next to a few swimmers and her natural racing streak magically and inevitably comes to the fore. As long as she doesn't get lost, she'll be fine!

I spot K in the queue for the race sign-on and join her. She's with a group of swimming friends and, as much as I'm tempted to pull her into my arms, all we can do is play it cool. We manage to convey a quick private, *I'm so desperately pleased to see you again. We've been too long apart (thirty-six and a half hours). When can I hold you? When can I kiss you?* look. We're given our race numbers that are written on the backs of our hands with an indelible marker pen. Mine is 22 and K's is 44.

08:15

The trip over to the start on the island is by ferry, and we manage to sit next to each other. I smuggle my hand beneath my towel and rest it lightly on her thigh. It's enough to feel grounded for a few seconds, to say silently, *Hello, I'm here. I'm back*. K looks over to me, her eyes shining brighter than ever, and sneaks her hand down to brush mine. I hope we're not attracting attention.

The one advantage of swimming around something solid like an island is that, in theory, you just keep turning left while keeping the island in view through the narrow, foggy tunnel of your goggles. Point-to-point races often result in a lot of meandering and it's easy to lose your bearings. Finding the *fastest* route around the island, however, is not a given. Too much indecision and you swim more metres than is necessary; swim too close to shore and you slow down, with the added risk of running aground – or worse, hitting something solid like a rock. Taking advantage of the tidal current is the fastest way to progress, which means working out where the deepest water is to maximise the 'push' of the current. But, of course, this only works in one's favour for half the race as, at the halfway point at Pottery Pier, the tide is usually against you. As can be the wind! And who knows what the sea state will be like. A small chop can be enough to cause breathing problems. Ironically, bigger, longer, more laggardly waves are easier to swim in; it's the small choppy stuff that makes it difficult to move efficiently. Then there is the cold. Even in August, the water can feel chilly – as we know, particularly if it takes a couple of hours or more to complete the event.

08:55

Five minutes until the start.

I run over to K – who's still chatting with her mates – and urge her to get a blinkin' move on!

'See you at the finish,' I say, 'and please do not overtake me. I would be most upset!'

I dive in and move my way up to the best position on the start line, treading water at the very far end, away from the mass of swimmers. My tactic is to hit it hard from the gun and stay in the deeper water for as long as possible before heading inshore as the island curves for the second time. Then, depending on where I'm positioned, draft my way up to the finish and, with 150 metres to go, sprint flat-out for the line. At least, that was the scenario I figured at last night. Today is race day – and who knows what will happen.

09:00

Bang! The gun goes and I sprint away as if it's a fifty-metre race. I look up quickly to check my trajectory, then it's head down and go like the clappers. After a couple of minutes, my lungs are bursting and I have to take in more oxygen fast, breathing every stroke as quickly as possible, if I'm to maintain any form or pace.

It already hurts in my chest and thighs, but I know if I don't keep pushing during this first section, then the chances of breaking free – finding smooth water undisturbed by other swimmers – will be curtailed. At the first 'corner' of the island, I decide to work out whether I should continue to stay out as far as possible in the deeper water, as per my original plan, or head into the shallower water and follow the slightly shorter route. I swim past a mooring buoy and check the speed of the water through the right lens of my goggles and am confident I'm doing the right thing by staying where I am. The flow is pretty good, even though most of the other swimmers are keeping close to shore. I think to myself how many times I have paddled in my kayak around Brownsea over the years. Countless times, and in all weathers and conditions. I know these waters and how they move. I keep pushing hard for the next fifteen minutes, then decide to cut across for the next 'corner' of the island. It's at this point in the race that my plan is to try to work out where I am, position-wise. To get my head up and out of the water and identify who is in front of me, or who is closing in from behind. Depending upon the outcome, I am either going to find a swimmer's feet to draft off or, if no one is about, work hard on my own and try not to get caught by anyone.

The halfway point appears, and I can see a handful of spectators' boats. A race official wants my number; they are anxious to check all the competitors are safe and fit to continue.

'Twenty-two,' I splutter.

'Well done, he's not far ahead. Keep going.'

Now, what does that mean, exactly? Is he referring to any old swimmer, or does he mean the *leader* is just ahead? I try not to let it niggle at me and make a conscious effort to clear my mind. I will have to wait until I'm able to get a clear view by lifting my chest out the water as high as possible off the top of a wave. I need to check the situation myself. I've done too many races over the years when well-meaning spectators shout something to you, only for it to be less than accurate or far from helpful. And the wrong thing said at the wrong moment can be completely demoralising.

I crack on, pushing as hard as I can while keeping my rhythm. Breathing every other stroke and doing a sighting stroke every five or six strokes to make sure I'm not wandering off course.

Now, I can see someone in front of me, but I am not sure whether there are others too. There are too many kayakers about, and they are blocking my already poor vision!

I decide to keep hammering at it as fast as I can. I do not want to get caught towards the end and I say to myself, *Take a look back with around four hundred metres to go, and if there is someone close, then sprint like buggery and get rid of them!*

I turn at the last corner and take a peek behind me. I can see a pair of fast-revolving arms about twenty metres away. Damn it! I pick up my pace a bit, wait a couple more minutes, then give it the full beans, sprinting flat-out until I cross the line. For a minute or more I am incapable of doing anything other than float on my back gasping for air. A friendly arm is tugging me closer to shore, but I'm in a world of pain and disorientation, to the point where I am not clear where the shore is. I rip off my goggles and try to lower my feet to the bottom but immediately find myself falling and floundering. The anonymous arm gently rights me. Slowly, as the lactic acid in my muscles abates and my oxygen levels return to normal, I regain my composure.

Someone taps me on the shoulder and says, 'Race number twenty-two? You've secured second!'

Phew! That's okay, I think. *But who was first?*

I wade ashore and there's a handshake and a pat on the back from the chap who beat me. 'Well done, mate, well done,' is all I can muster, and I go and grab a fizzy drink to remove the over-salty taste from my mouth. Once recovered a little, I watch the other swimmers coming in and look for K.

Where is she? Did she turn left or right at the halfway point? How is she? I continue to look down the field of swimmers as more and more arrive, in varying states of exhaustion. One guy can barely crawl from the water and volunteers wade out to help him. *Was I that bad? No! Can't have been. At least, I don't think so.*

I keep on looking down towards the last corner in the hope of seeing K, and there she is. K's unmistakable seagull wing-like swim stroke, as her leading arm goes slightly wide but has a gentle kink in it. It *is* so like a black-backed gull or a herring gull's wing. She's right in the middle of a pack of five other swimmers and they're all going for it. It will be a sprint for the line!

My heart is racing as I watch them fight it out over the last one hundred metres. K is leading the group, but only just. On her left is someone big and strong with quite an aggressive stroke and to her right another girl who has a very fast turnover rate. K, with her longer, rangier stroke, is just about staying ahead and I wonder if she knows exactly where the finish line is.

I start shouting. 'Go! Go! Go! Sprint!' But it is useless of course, as it is almost impossible to hear anything with so much splashing and twirling of arms and legs. K hangs on and leads the group in by just a couple of metres. I rush into the water, swim over to her and grabbing her arms, help her up.

'I'm so proud of you. I'm so proud of you,' I say, while she coughs and splutters.

'Is this the finish?' she gabbles. 'Is this the end?'

'Yes, yes, it is,' I laugh. 'This *is* the finish. I'm just so proud of you,' I say again.

I help her from the water; she can barely stand. We arrive at the drinks station and she downs a large glass of lemonade. By now she's recovering, and her matchless smile is returning.

10:45

'I think you did really, really well,' I say. 'I'm pretty sure you are one of the top women finishers.'

'No! Surely not. There seemed to be a lot of people ahead of me.'

'You might well be surprised.'

We generally socialise and soak up the post-race feeling, something that is quite addictive. A sense of euphoria related to having risen to a challenge and completed it. You and your body against Mother Nature. A unique and glorious buzz.

12:00

Prize giving and plaudits over, K says she needs to make a call. She must clarify whether she needs to leave right away or can hang around for another couple of hours. I pray it's the latter, as I am desperate to tell her something. Today is the day.

12:15

'All sorted! They're all quite happy at the beach. I'm okay for a couple of hours.'

'Let's nip over on the ferry then and grab some food at the café-restaurant. Remember the place?'

'I should think so!'

'Let's go. There's not a moment to lose!'

We sneak away and head to the place where we had our first meal together. Followed by our moon-lit skinny-dip.

At the café, we're both still on a high. K is excitedly retelling the story of her race. For now, I'm content to listen. To watch her animated joy.

Except there is one thing, an important thing, that needs to be said. I felt it first this morning (again) when I awoke.

'I have something I want to say to you.' I reach for her hand across the table.

'What is it?'

'It's—'

I slide my left hand further into K's right hand, and K looks down at them. She is studying our hands with a look of studied concentration that is at odds with the mundanity of our familiar grip. I tilt my head and when she lifts her head, I gaze into her eyes.

'Look! Look,' she says excitedly. 'Our hands. The numbers twenty-two and forty-four.'

We still have our race numbers, not yet washed away by the sea.

'Don't you see? Don't you see? "One's not half two. It's two are halves of one".'

I take a few seconds to work out what she means.

'Our numbers. Twenty-two and forty-four. One is half of the other.' She is almost transcendent with joy.

'Of course, of course. "One's not half two. It's two are halves of one",' I repeat slowly. 'E. E. Cummings again?'

'Yes, of course. But isn't it just heavenly? How good is that, twenty-two and forty-four. Hah!'

'It is when you know what I want to say to you.' I laugh too loudly. Enough for me to do a quick 360 to make sure I haven't upset anyone else in the café.

'What, what are you going to tell me?'

'I wanted to tell you last week, when we were on our secret bathing ledges, but something got in the way.'

'Really?'

'It's something quite simple.'

I lean towards her and take hold of both her hands.

'I love you,' I say quickly. 'I. Love. You. I'm *in* love with you.'

K's face is frozen. She looks in pain and has an intensity about her that I've not seen before.

She forcibly pulls my hands towards her so they are resting on her chest. Her grip is unnaturally fierce, and her nails are digging into my skin.

She whispers, 'But don't you know? Can't you see? I've been telling you *that for weeks*!'

For a moment the world stands still. Then we both laugh out loud. It's as if we've just been told the funniest joke of our lives. My stomach muscles begin to hurt.

Suddenly, things have become serious. Now, surely, is the time to kiss this woman. The woman I love.

I stand up, lean over the table, pull her towards me and K offers her salt-encrusted sexy lips. Instantly, the world restarts; and beyond it a very big door has just opened, welcoming us through – to a whole new un-travelled landscape.

Monday 16th August

09:15
22+44°
Grin size: XXL
K outlook: ↑ ↑
Office forecast: ↑
Exercise outlook: Too wrecked!

Oh, how my body aches. I'm as stiff as a board, but still I proudly wear my race number 22 on the back of my hand.

Sent a number of text messages to 44 this morning to check whether she is still in one piece and relatively pain free – unlike me.

<I was just checking the phone when it vibrated! I'm in no pain. Only in my heart>

09:30
Last night, alone and tucked up under the covers, I couldn't help wondering – when will the numbers 22 + 44 finally become 2424?

09:35
I'm so desperately keen to talk about K to my friends and family; about this incredible person I've met. But I dare not. The stakes remain too high right now. We are a secret, and for now, it must remain that way.

Have nearly completed my latest poem for K in tribute to our week on the Purbeck. I do hope she likes it.

Wednesday 18th August

08:00
GBR have five golds!
Office forecast: ↑

The big phone is ringing. It's Lois.

Me: 'Would the caller please identify herself.'

Lois: 'Very funny. Where the bloody hell have you been?'

Me: 'Racing! I got a good result last weekend and I'm really pleased with the result – second place; it just all seemed to come together – other than I just couldn't catch the guy out in front!'

Lois: 'Oh! I've been trying to get hold of you… anyway, very well done for that! You need to remember though, you're getting on a bit now, you're no spring chicken… so you can't be expected to win races all the time. What age was the chap who won?'

Me: 'Hmm. 'Bout twenty-three.'

Lois: 'And you are…?'

Me: 'Yes, but I don't want to start using age as an excuse, otherwise that'll be on my mind when I'm on the start line and I may as well give up then and there!'

Lois: 'Are you racing this weekend or… what are you doing? It's been ages since I last saw you?'

Me: 'Er. Um. Just training, I think. What you doing?'

Lois: 'Well, I will be finishing this job by Friday with luck, then I have a few things to do Saturday and so, what about if I came over for Saturday evening and maybe we can head out somewhere… or perhaps stay in?'

Me: 'Yes – er – yes – er, that would be, er – ideal. Saturday night, and we'll do something. Then chill out on Sunday, perhaps?'

Lois: 'Wonderful plan. See you then. Be good. Byeeeeee.'

I put the phone down and instantly feel a big knot tightening up in my tummy. I don't like doing this to her.

'Be good,' she says.

Argh!

09:30

<Meet today?>

09:35

<With the children. Call me please. Safe to talk>

10:48

Tim is off on some photography course for a couple of days, then he is back to work. K is being mum again and on duty.

Have told her I have something for her – my poem – but it looks like it will be swim training tomorrow night before I can hand it over. She said she's working on a few things. By that she means she is trying to arrange some free time…

10:55

Need to bury my head in some office work urgently and change my focus. There is quite a lot I should be getting on with and I'm so behind on it all.

Thursday 19th August

09:20
F2-3 perfect!
K forecast: ↑
Office forecast: ↑
Exercise outlook: ↑

Just back off the water from an early morning paddle. Five of us, and the extra numbers made for a pleasant change. Felt really strong in the boat and have so much surplus energy which I can't seem to burn off! Looking forward to swim training tonight.

11:30

<Meet tonight earlier at six? Can you?>

<Yes. C u there. Can't wait to hold you>

<Me too!!!>

17:50
At the pool.

My stomach hurts: K has this effect on me. When I've not seen her for a day or more, the anticipation, the pure excitement, is sufficiently great to induce physical symptoms. As soon as I'm with her they dissipate, but waiting for her, knowing I'm going to see her, is like the ten minutes before the start of a big race.

'Hello.' A hand rests softly on my shoulder.

She's crept up on me in the coffee bar.

I kiss her on the cheek, and it feels totally bloody weird. I want to grab her, wrap my arms around her, push her to the floor and – but we're in a public place where there are small children and grown-up people with serious-looking faces. We'd get thrown out.

'Quick cup of tea, then the squash courts?'

K smiles and nods. 'A quick one… yes!' she says, and laughs. Her thinking is clearly on the same wavelength as mine.

18:05

I'm trying to drink my tea quickly but it's really hot –annoyingly so, and all I can do is sip it. K, on the other hand, seems to have an armour-plated gullet and is halfway through hers already.

18:25

She's in my arms at last, at last, at last. And what a wonderful, rejuvenating feeling it is. My arms have felt useless these last four days without her wrapped inside them, and now she's back! I absorb K as much as I am able and soak her in. This is my paradise.

'Read me your poem,' she whispers softly in my ear. 'I like it when you read to me.'

'Of course.'

Reading poetry out loud at the back of a sweaty squash court is probably the least ideal surroundings one could aspire to, but beggars and choosers and all that.

'I'll pretend we're sitting next to a gently flowing chalk stream while holding hands on a brilliant late-spring-like day.'

'Very good idea. I'm with you. Actually, you need to picture where we were last week – our secret bathing ledges. Keep it in mind, as this is about *that* afternoon.'

seaside kisses

kissing you reminds me of places electric
in the summer sun of amber and the blue
and dried white sea – on brows and cheeks
all over you;
of wispy horses too frisky in to play
on bathing ledges all so secret—mustn't say
the water.

kissing you reminds me of sweet life-breath
with eye locked moments
and forehead kisses,
entangled ribbons of sun-streaked hair
and giddy heads–
and seagulls happy just to stare
the breeze.

kissing you reminds me of locked filled fingers
into curves and tightness
ten-sed in the linger
(warmth – so hot),
and just to be, to listen – not prevaricate,
with moments that insatiate
the silence.

'That's really lovely. I was immediately transported back there again. We *must* return soon.'

'Absolutely, while the weather is still good. Let me know when you can be free, and we'll get down there for an afternoon or more.'

'I'm working on a few things for next week, just waiting to hear back from people… and then we can be together,' she declares.

K pauses.

'You know, I've written you a letter. I have it here – in my bag.'

'Brilliant! Brilliant! You must read it to me before swimming. We still have time.'

K hands me an envelope with a big 22 in her neat penmanship on the front. I slide my finger along the top, trying not to rip the paper too much, pull out the letter, unfold it, and hand it back to K.

Like a mother reading to her child, she lets the words flow over me.

Wednesday
(A good sea breeze)

Within the circuit of this plodding life
There enter moments of an azure hue
(Henry David Thoreau)

Dear 22,

Since writing to you last, have felt much better. No idea why, except that seeing you keeps me going, though the effect wears off rapidly, so roll on the next time (soon please).

Apart from the way you look, smell, taste and feel (and in particular your nose, the lines on your smiling face, your profile in the car, your hands and your brown bare feet), I adore the way you hold my gaze – and when combined with jammers and a swim cap – the effect is intensified…! The fact that you can laugh and cry, eat straight from the fridge, do things one handed, makes me melt. I adore your words. The way you write and all the times I see '1 message received'. I adore it when you lose your glasses and I can find them. I understand all of you (I think), and you see more in me than I see in myself. I am in awe of your self-control (for where would we be without that!). You deserve a medal.

But most of all, I like the part of you that sacrificed the boredom most of us succumb to in order to be true to yourself. To simply… enjoy… is not always the easiest path.

And do you know what you have given me?

Stars, sea-cliff camping, sleeping bag heaven, white bed, green hill, falling asleep in your arms, sea freedom, sea swims, kisses on the top of the hill, crying together, playing in the water, pieces of wood, smooth stones in pockets, words, you astride my kayak, poetry, numbers, touch, kindness, honesty, hearing you say you were so proud of me after my swim and, finally, the incredible feel of one another turning in the dark and clinging together ever more tightly, as if fearful of losing grip and letting go. And, then in the morning do nothing but looking – and talking of what we might yet do…

I realise my own passion is equally matched by your passion.

I love you so much.
PS. You have shown me how to play once more.
PPS. You kept using the 'we' word last Sunday am – did u know?

'Damnation! You've got me,' I say, fighting back the tears. 'How do you do it, you've got me. All of me.'

We hold each other for a while, then I feel K lift her head. She looks at me unblinking and says, irrefutably, 'You and I make a "we" and that's how it *must* be.'

'Yes, I concur. We are a "we". Most definitely.'

Friday 20th August

11:30

I'm sitting nervously in the emergency dentist's waiting room for pain relief of a recalcitrant molar and thumbing through the only available magazine – a dog-eared copy of *Women's Realm*.

I see a rather lame article on 'new relationships' that happens to catch my eye. A Mr P Robinson from Milton Keynes has written a letter to the editor extolling the wonders of finding his true love. His words grab my attention.

Urgently, I tap them into my phone and then send them off in a text to K:

> *<If this person (you find) doesn't want to make you rip all your hair out, change your name, or move to a foreign country, then you don't have a relationship, you have a hobby...>*

A short while later, K, obviously on a similar wave of thinking:

> *<If you only look at what is, you might never attain what could be>*

It seems wherever I look, words of meaning abound and their poignancy seems oh-so relevant to the moment.

Friday 20th August

FIVE DAYS LATER

Wednesday 25th August

11:00
Not rained in ages +19°
9 Gold medals now!
Work forecast:↑
Exercise outlook: ↑

It's K's birthday on Saturday and I have found her the perfect boat. She has suggested on more than one occasion she would love a kayak of her own, and now I can make it a reality. I've paid the deposit and it will be ready to collect on Friday – in time for her birthday. It will be a contest to see who is the more excited!

11:30

<Meet for ten mins today?>

<Yes but tricky. Only if you want to come shopping. Waitrose 1pm?>

<OK. See u by the malt loaf>

13:05
I'm loitering in the bakery aisle and feeling somewhat self-conscious. There are people who have recognised me, and the security staff are on alert as I'm hovering in the busiest area of the supermarket not doing very much. I've already been approached by two members of the swim club who were 'surprised to see me in here', and an old cycling friend who said I looked lost. There's no sign of K nor a text from her, so I

must presume I've either got the wrong supermarket or she's been held up somewhere.

I decide to leave the malt loaf department and go for a wander among the breakfast cereals. I turn the corner at the bottom of the aisle and, hooray, there's K. But not just K. Mini K too! This is a first. Mum and daughter together, holding hands. My goodness, they look delightful next to each other.

K's not seen me yet; she's bent down talking to Anna, who seems quite keen on the assorted dried fruit display and is pointing to something exotic. I'm smiling everywhere. I want this moment to endure, so I back up a bit. I don't want to be seen too quickly; this is fascinating. Anna has stopped again, this time at the yoghurt counter. She clearly likes the look of them. K patiently squats down and is saying something. Anna smiles and then they move on. I try to back up even more but am running out of room. I decide to head back to the bakery section and act surprised at their (imminent) arrival.

'Ah-ha. Here you are!' I say and throw my arms up in the air pretending to act surprised.

'And who is this?' I bend down. 'So, what is your name, young lady?'

'I'm Anna,' she reluctantly admits, then looks up at K as if to say, *Who is this person, Mummy*?

'Nice to meet you, Anna. I'm a swimming friend of Mummy's.'

She stares at me nonplussed.

I look at K, who's smiling at us. 'Don't worry. We've had a bit of an up and down morning.' She turns to Anna. 'We're taking you to your best friend's after this, aren't we? You're going to play together.'

'Lucky girl,' I say. 'Wish I could come along!'

I wander a few more aisles with the two of them. I watch Anna as much as I dare, obsessed by the way she moves and by her engaging facial expressions. Both are identical to K's and I can't stop smiling inside.

'You okay?' I whisper.

'Yes. But I *need* to see you.'

'When?'

'Friday, midday onwards. I think I've got it organised now.'

'You'll come over to me?'

'Yes.'

'I have something for you.'

'Oh! Really?'

'Is it safe to give it to you now, or I can keep it until swim training tomorrow?'

'No, now is good. Slip it into my side pocket.'

I smuggle the small brown discreet-looking envelope into her pocket along with a pebble from Shell Bay beach I found while paddling. It's white, smooth, ovoid; somehow deeply pleasurable to hold.

We wander the aisles like two languid grazing gazelles before I admit I should be heading off back to my home office. I turn towards the exit.

'Bye, Anna. It's been lovely to meet you,' I say, waving.

'Bye-bye,' she shouts, and then frantically waves back with both hands.

ONE DAY LATER

Friday 27th August

08:40
Blue. F2-3 SW
***Blue Peter* homework: ↑**

I began it last night and must say, so far I'm rather proud of myself. I've made a boat with my own hands, using only primitive tools to create a model fit for the National Maritime Museum. When I say model, I mean a *par excellence* example of origami.

While it may be crafted from photocopier paper and card robbed from a Do Not Bend envelope, it is a perfect rendition of K's real birthday gift: a top-of-the-range sea kayak, just like mine.

09:45
I'm applying the finishing touches to the paper-and-card kayak using my best crayoning skills (isn't colouring fun!), adding detail to the deck. To fabricate K as the paddler, I've shaped a piece of driftwood for her body, a lump of Blu-Tack for her head, used some of her hair (collected up from my bedroom floor!), toothpicks for her arms, and made a paddle out of a coffee stirrer. To construct the blades, I've used slightly thicker paper shaped using 'a good pair of sensible Safety Scissors', as Valerie Singleton used to advise. The whole ensemble is held together with white paper glue.

The plan is to give it to K as her pretend birthday present.

There's only one problem: the real kayak has yet to turn up. It should have been here an hour ago but has yet to show...

10:30

Panic over. The boat has arrived and I'm unpacking it like it's mine. It is beautiful, and I know K will adore it. I mean, what girl wouldn't want their very own self-powered water transport: a vehicle for discovering new worlds and experiencing fresh wild adventures.

12:30

K has arrived and is examining me with studied curiosity. She can read me a mile off and knows something is afoot.

'What is it? What's going on? You're not holding me like you usually do.'

'Come this way. Follow me.'

I lead K into the sitting room and sit her down on the sofa, then hand her my gift wrapped in a box the size of a shoe box (actually, it is an old cycling shoe box, but she'll be fine with it).

'Happy birthday, number 44!'

'But it's not until tomorrow! What is it? A pair of shoes? New flip-flops?'

K shakes the box but can't hear anything rattle. She tears off the wrapping paper with gusto.

'Not shoes. Take a peek inside.'

K lifts the lid, moves the tissue paper aside, and her face lights up – before she roars with laughter.

'A model kayak! How brilliant! And is that me? What a likeness! I could put it on my desk at work maybe, or somewhere else safe. As long as no one touches it, of course.'

'Best not to touch it too much! It's a little delicate and not really fit for the sea!'

I'm staring at her, grinning. Relishing her evident pleasure and unfeigned amusement.

'What?' she says suspiciously.

'I've got something I want to show you.'

I take K's hand and walk with her out of the house and across to the garage side door. I open it and flip on the strip lights. We wait while they painstakingly flicker into action.

I've wrapped a large pink ribbon all the way around the hull and written 44 across the bow. K looks at me in wide-eyed disbelief.

'This is my proper gift for you,' I say, pointing to the kayak. 'Happy birthday, sweetheart.'

'Eh? Mine? This… is… really for me? My *own* boat?'

'Yes, it's yours. Identical in almost every respect to my orange one, but in cobalt blue.'

'Wow.'

K walks around the front of the kayak, running her hands down the glossy deck, taking a peek inside the cockpit, and opening up the hatches. She inhales the newness of the boat.

'Such a lovely smell. I could almost get high on it alone! When can we go out?' she says, hopping from one foot to the other. 'Is there time today? What about Monday, or Tuesday, or next Friday afternoon?'

'Whenever you can make it. We'll go off somewhere and I'll take you to places you've never seen before.'

'I'm sure you will. I simply can't wait. It's *sooo* beautiful. *My* blue boat. I really can't quite believe it.'

13:40

We head back inside the house and I make us a cup of tea. After a while I say, 'Let's go upstairs.'

'Yes, but I've only got a couple of hours.'

I hold out my hand and she takes it. Eagerly, we walk to the bottom of the stairs. I scoop her up effortlessly into my arms and we climb the stairs. I kick the bedroom door shut, and entwined, we tumble softly onto the bed.

17:25

<I fell apart at the crossroads. You, my blue birthday boats, your lovingness... all too much. (And I was so happy – just with your paper model!)>

19:25

A little later.

I return to my office desk I see K has scribbled out a little note, and left it on my pad:

'Spending time with you is like seeing earth from space'

I know exactly what she means. It is like we are floating the whole time, looking down upon each other from above, being a part of the scene but also being a spectator as well. Even when apart, I often feel I'm watching her – looking down from on high, seeing her every move, sometimes from quite a low height, maybe twenty feet or so and sometimes from a very great height, hundreds of feet high. It is a little like taking the roof off a doll's house and looking into the rooms, seeing everything in detail in one large frame.

It's something very surreal but incredibly beautiful at the same time.

Saturday 28th August

11:00
Middling, +18°
In the pool.

Birthday girl was on top form in the water today and I couldn't beat her at backstroke or butterfly! We played our usual games, swimming side by side in adjoining lanes, trying to brush hands, bump bums, or touch one another's thighs. Not always easy to do with thirty other swimmers. Think I may have accidentally felt Rachel's thigh in lane two a couple of times, but pretty sure she won't have minded.

Sometimes I feel it's as intimate as taking a proper bath with her: electric, passionate and dangerous, despite being in the presence of others, sneaking glances through the corners of our goggles.

When she finishes the set, I watch as her legs sink slowly to the bottom of the pool where they rest with her feet in the perfect duck-pointed poise. She leans against the wall as if inviting me in. When she pushes off for the next set, I reach out and try to brush my fingers along the length of her cossie and then her thigh. When she returns, I try to stand next to her, my thigh rubbing up against her hip and my hand down by my side out of view, frantically seeking to interlock with hers. Once found, I squeeze her fingers tightly and she responds, relieved by our reunion after minutes of swim-set separation.

The session is nearly finished now, and the group is mingling at the shallow end.

I catch Ann mischievously smiling at me; I can tell something's up – she's always up to no good! Have our underwater caresses been spotted?

Ann moves over to where I'm standing. 'Turn around,' she demands, rather too loudly.

'Eh?'

'Turn around, I want to take a look at your back.'

I rotate slowly while wondering what the heck it is she is going to do to me.

She places the tips of her fingers on the sides of my back and draws them slowly downwards a few inches. Ouch! It's surprisingly painful.

'Just as I thought,' she says, 'looks like the cat has scratched your back!'

'Whaaat…?'

I spin back around to face her and discover Ann and Rachel in fits of laughter. K immediately submerges herself underwater and does not want to be seen! We've been rumbled. Oops!

'Yeah,' I say, with as much innocence as I can muster, 'I really must get her claws trimmed.'

Which only prompts another fit of giggles, so I slink away with my tail between my legs and go to find K, who's disappeared somewhere down the deep end.

Sunday 29th August

07:00

F3-4 SW +19°

Yes, we were exposed yesterday by our swimming friends, but I'm hoping those two will keep it to themselves. Over the years I've heard rumours about other people at the club and their clandestine relationships, but no one seemed that fussed. A bit of gossip here and there, but the banter is always light-hearted and none too snide that I've ever heard.

My issue today is that I'm due at Lois's for lunch and was going to stay over. If I go, I will just have to keep my shirt on and/or turn the lights off.

Not good.

Monday 30th August

09:00
Office forecast: Open & Graham's back
K outlook: ↑

I received a bit of a lecture just now from an old friend, indeed a very good old friend. In the long phone call, she managed to extract from me the details of my current situation. To be honest, it wasn't difficult for her. I blabbed willingly, eager to tell her of this amazing person I've met who is changing my life in an instant and with such ease.

The conversation brought to the forefront of my mind something that's been very well boxed up until now; K's marriage and her three lovely children. Oh, and K's husband Tim. And oh, the collateral damage that can be caused when a family is torn apart. There are so many painful aspects of this… and I should know. My parents split up when I was five years old and I grew up being shuttled between two parents, spending time with adults I could not know and generally living in a state of quiet confusion and personal isolation.

The thought of *me* causing such potential trauma to others shudders me with grief.

11:30
Text from K.

> *<When... when... when?>*

She's been texting me this morning as she wants to have a go in her new boat one afternoon this week.

I'm struggling to say no.

11:50
Another text from K.

<Would you like company this Thursday night? Paddle Friday am?>

I give in.

<Er... yeah!!!>

<Think I can work it. Will confirm>

<OK. Discuss tonight before swim. Meet early?>

<Yes>

SEPTEMBER

'I look at you and I see me'

Friday 3rd September

06:30
Blue and bright +18°

I awake this morning to the best pair of eyes and the most beautiful face I have ever seen, and my back and sides have happy memory marks almost their entire length.

I can't think of a better way to express the wonders from last night than with the following twelve words… or should it be just the one!

Warmth, touch, breath, scent, eyes, hair, skin, lips, stars, views, floating, white linen, warmth, touch, breath, scent, eyes, hair, skin, lips, stars, views, floating, white linen, warmth, touch, breath, scent, eyes, hair, skin, lips, stars, views, floating, white linen, warmth, touch, breath, scent, eyes, hair, skin, lips, stars, views, floating, white linen, warmth, touch, breath, scent, eyes, hair, skin, lips, stars, views, floating, white linen, warmth, touch, breath, scent, eyes, hair, skin, lips, stars, views, floating, white linen, warmth, touch, breath, scent, eyes, hair, skin, lips, stars, views, floating, white linen, warmth, touch, breath, scent, eyes, hair, skin, lips, stars, views, floating, white linen, warmth, touch, breath, scent, eyes, hair, skin, lips, stars, views, floating, white linen, E-N-T-W-I-N-E-M-E-N-T!

A night to remember, for sure. Made even more incredible this morning when K crept downstairs to make us large mugs of tea but seemed to be an age. When she finally snuck back under the duvet, she was grinning widely.

'What have you been up to?' I ask.

'Oh, nothing.'

'Yes, you have. I can tell. What have you done downstairs? I'm going to take a look.'

I wander into the kitchen, hallway and around the sitting room, but can't see anything particularly obvious – but when I take a peek through the garden windows, K's early morning handiwork is plain to see!

Laid out along the length of the garden table are the windblown petals from the pink rose bush, artfully arranged in four big letters. The petals spell out the word L O V E.

I run back upstairs and jump on top of her laughing, shaking the bed up and down with my hands.

'You are so amazing,' I say. 'How do you do it… I just can't tell you enough how much I love you so, so, very, very much, I really do.'

'I love you too. I don't want this to ever end.'

How fantastic!

08:50

We're loading the kayaks onto the car roof rack. K's new all-blue boat is next to my trusty orange one, and they look great together! K's so excited, and I can't help thinking how I wish little Anna and the boys were here to witness their mum acting as if she were their age.

'Damn. I forgot to bring some champagne along for the big launch,' I joke. 'We need to break something over the bow.'

K rummages through her rucksack and pulls out a drinks can.

'How about All Natural Orange Juice (with no added flavourings)?'

'Perfect, who needs fake fizz, anyhow? Your kayak is more the organic type, anyway.'

09:30

We're at the water's edge ready to get going and K has the juice in her hand. She prises the can open and delivers her speech.

'I name this ship *Mine*. May God bless all who paddle her. Hip, hip hooray!'

'Hooray!' I add.

We set off with the tide and head down past Brownsea Island towards the harbour entrance. K is immediately at home in her boat and full of talk of expeditions.

'Maybe we could take the boats for a long kayaking trip to the Scilly Isles. It is supposed to be beautiful there, and then perhaps over to Lundy and perhaps along the Pembroke coast? We could also go whale watching from them – in the Sea of Cortez too. What do you think?'

'We could!'

'I'd love to see some whales from this boat. Imagine seeing a fifty- or sixty-foot sperm whale or humpback whale right up close and then to see them breach in front of us! It would be incredible!'

'It would!'

'Imagine if we saw pods of dolphins, too, leaping along with me as I paddle, side by side, cresting above the surface and then disappearing below. Only to appear again right alongside. It would be beyond wonderful.'

'It would!'

'We could go on camping trips; load the boats up with kit in these hatches and then head off and spend long nights together snuggled up on a beach somewhere. We could paddle down to Ringstead again and spend another night under the stars.'

'We could!'

'Why don't we put some dates aside now and get the planning going?'

'We should!'

'Actually, I should probably practise my capsize drill a bit more, just in case I should go over… and I think I need to get a better windproof top as this one is not very good. And some better paddling shoes, and…'

'You should!'

K's off in a world of her own; such things happen easily when out on the water in one's boat. We paddle steadily around the remaining islands before heading back towards the beach.

11:55

'I love what you do for me,' K says as we come off the water. 'I love the sheer simplicity of all this,' she says, pointing at the water. 'The immersion in, the exploration of, our natural environment.'

'Wait until we do one of the trips you were mentioning earlier, then you really feel part of nature!' I say.

'Well, that's something to look forward to when I'm back at work next week!'

'We just have to make sure it happens.'

13:50

K has gone and I'm cleaning down the boats.

A text comes through.

<'I ought to say,' explained Pooh as they walked down to the shore of the Island, 'that it isn't just an ordinary sort of boat. Sometimes it's a boat, and sometimes it's more of an accident. It all depends.' 'Depends on what?' said Piglet. 'On whether I'm on top of it or underneath it!'>

Then, a little later on, I get this which has me chuckling:

<I drove the car into a hedge! My mind was elsewhere – still with you – and I completely missed the corner! I'm ok but Tim is furious with me for damaging the car... but it's nothing really>

Classic!

01:45

Unable to sleep.

Now that we have declared – the very obvious – to one another, the issues of our circumstance are coming to the fore.

The words, *What are we going to do?* have been bouncing around my head for weeks and weeks but it is apparent now the issues are really mounting. This 'thing' that we both thought we could 'go with' and try to 'put out of our system', is now too firmly sealed and not ever for expediting (that is for certain).

I check my phone and see a text from K:

<You have put a spell on me. Pls arrange for a happy ending>

Guess she is having similar concerns.

Saturday 4th September

10:25

Swim training is nearly over, and K has just told me that her children are waiting in the café. I can meet them before they all go off to see the grandparents for the weekend. Tim, it seems, has gone into town.

10:35

I walk upstairs to the coffee bar and there are three little people sitting obediently around a table. Two of them have their heads busy in a colouring book, and the other, Robert, is tapping his foot against the chair leg while casually watching everyone.

K crosses straight over to the table. All three of them look up and Michael and Anna lift up their books to show her their artistic efforts.

K comes over to where I'm standing at the counter, smiling.

'All okay?' I ask.

'Oh yes, they're fine. Glenn kept them occupied while I got dressed.' Glenn is a solid muscular swimmer – all brute force and little finesse, but a charmer and at times, very funny.

Right now, he is joking with Anna, who is fascinated by the grotesque size of his leg muscles – complete with a set of scars from a particularly gruesome skiing accident involving a tree in the wrong place. Glenn is spinning one of his horrid yarns that the kids are lapping up.

Now it's Anna's turn, and she tells everyone her recently learnt new joke.

'Why was six scared?'

'Dunno,' we all say in harmony. 'Why was six scared?'

'Because (long pause) seven ate nine!'

Everyone laughs and Glenn claps.

'Okay, I've got a joke,' I say. 'You'll like this one. Ready?'

'Yes,' Anna says.

'What are caterpillars afraid of?'

'Um… I don't know.'

'Dogerpillars!'

Anna pulls a face. 'That's silly!'

Tough audience.

Another member of the club, sat at the nearest table, leans over and says he has a joke too.

'What did the Spanish fireman call his two sons?'

Anna looks at him expectantly.

'Hose A and hose B.'

Anna fails to laugh, but the rest of us chortle.

'Jose is a Spanish boy's name,' he carefully explains to Anna. She looks at him with all the superiority only a six-year-old girl can muster.

'Well, I'm not learning Spanish yet.'

Unarguable. Suitably chastised, the failed joke-teller returns to his half-drunk coffee.

10:50

Suddenly the look on K's face changes significantly.

Tim is standing at the top of the stairs signalling impatiently that it's time to go.

I slump down onto a seat and prepare to be a spectator from chair level height.

'C'mon you three, drink up,' K says, hurrying them along.

She glances over to me and I raise my eyebrows.

I stare at K's back and, at the top of the stairs, as Tim disappears she turns quickly and looks into my eyes. I give a single flick of my head, as if to say, *It's all cool, Mary Poppins, everything's fine. Be safe, stay out of trouble, enjoy your children, enjoy time with your parents, speak to you later, look forward to seeing you on Monday, miss you already, wish you were in my arms permanently, my heart is with you, I love you.*

10:55

I grab another coffee, chat with the guys for a while longer, then make my way out. I'm competing tomorrow, so it's time to go and find my race head. Lois is coming over tonight. I ought to tidy the house. And find my Lois head, come to think of it.

EIGHT DAYS LATER

Sunday 12th September

16:00
All blue, thank you +23°

> *<Accommodating visitors for tea?>*

> *<Yes! Come right over. I'm here now>*

Unusually for a Sunday, K's coming over. I'm sensing something isn't quite right, or maybe today I just got lucky?

16:15
As I open the front door, K thumps into my arms with more force than usual and buries her head under my shoulder. She's holding me very tightly.

'I've missed you so much today,' she murmurs. 'Just hold me in your arms.'

We reverse back into the sitting room, waddling like a duck with four legs, and fall back onto the sofa. She nestles herself into me and I feel her breathing gradually slow to a gentle idle. She is completely tranquil and within minutes I sense she has fallen asleep.

The house is still: noise is absent as if we've been transported back to an eighteenth-century Sabbath in the wilds of Dorset. Even the birds seem to have retreated to an unusual quietude this afternoon. All I can hear is K's rhythmic, gentle susurrations. For now, the world has yet again kindly agreed to stand still.

A while ago, K told me she has always slept on the edge of the marital bed, facing a big window. Tim lies in the centre facing in the opposite direction, and they only come together irregularly and sporadically to make love. She says they have always slept like this and it's not something she's ever thought was untoward.

I was shocked. I inwardly compare it to how we are when together. It's as if we are welded together, face to face, and turn as one through the night. For either of us to part from the other during the night engenders a sense of panic not unlike the disconcerting falling sensation of nightmares.

17:45

'Crikey, how long have I been asleep?' K says, suddenly awaking and looking at the clock.

'You were out for the count. You've not been sleeping properly the last few days?'

'Not very well. Certainly not a full night.'

I notice a mark just above her right wrist and, lifting up the short sleeve of her tee-shirt, a bruise on her arm.

'How did you get those?'

'Not sure. With kids you're always banging into things.'

'This one looks like a wrist burn. I used to get them at the numerous schools I went to. New boy syndrome. Stung like hell.'

K isn't saying anything and lies impassive on my chest. Something is wrong and my mind, rebelliously independent, is reluctant to go there.

'Whatever you knocked your arm against, it must have been quite a blow. That is going to be a sizeable bruise.'

'Oh, it was just one of those silly accidents.'

'A silly accident?'

'Yes!'

'This mark on your wrist – an accident too?' I ask, carefully tracing the reddened outline with my forefinger.

'Just one of those things. It's nothing, really.'

'Doesn't look like nothing to me, looks painful.'

'Like I say, all's fair in love and war when you are trying to manage three fractious kids cooped up in the house!'

K's head still rests on my chest and I can see her eyes are tightly shut.

'You'd tell me if things got… heavy at home, wouldn't you?'

There's a pause. I repeat my question.

'Wouldn't you?'

K gives a brief single nod but says nothing, her eyes still firmly closed.

Then she suddenly pipes up. 'Hey, I'd love a cuppa. Can I have it in one of your big pint mugs? Then I must get back, I'm on taxi duty again.'

'Of course, you may. I'll go and put the kettle on right this instant.'

18:00

K's gone.

I return to the sofa and try to figure out what might be happening. Is Tim really the kind of man to inflict physical abuse on his wife? And if so, how long has it been going on?

A *big* red flag has been hoisted and I must be very alert to what's potentially going on here. This kind of thing is categorically unacceptable. Unacceptable.

Argh!

Monday 13th September

11:00
F2-3, SW +18°
Office forecast: ↑
Exercise outlook: ↑

Work head is very much on this week. Graham and I are off to a trade show in Holland for two days, flying out on Wednesday morning at some very early hour and then getting back late Friday night. Should be manageable. I've yet to inform K but will do so tonight. Am concerned about her after what I saw yesterday and have been thinking about it. It's a topic I can discuss with Graham when we're away, as he's bound to have a few opinions on the subject.

Received two lovely texts, however, from K first thing this morning.

> *<I now know 'that love is worth the time it takes to find.' Think of that>*

Followed by:

> *<I love you to bits>*

I replied with:

> *<It isn't so much the wanting to be with as not wanting to be without>*

Tuesday 14th September

09:00
F5, SW +18°

Goddamn it! Seriously, what the hell?

K's just left a distressed-sounding message on my phone. Desperate for me to call her back as soon as I can.

I'm trying 'our' phone, but it is endlessly going to voicemail.

Balls!

I've sent a text.

<I'm here. Are you OK? What's happened?>

But nothing has come back yet.

What do I do?

I'll give it another thirty minutes and if I've still heard nothing, I will drive to her house.

09:32

It's K! Calling at last!

Me: 'Are you okay? What's happened?'

K: (She is in tears.) 'Yes, yes, I'm okay.'

Me: 'What is it? Are you hurt?'

K: 'Only in my heart. I am fearful.'

Me: 'What has you frightened?'

K: 'Us. I fear for us.'

Me: (Silently.) *Oh shit, shit, shit!*

K: 'It's him. Tim. He's gone off on one.'

Me: 'Why?'

K: 'He found some texts on the phone, the other phone. I meant to delete all of them, but, well, I so hate doing it and then forgot. He got very upset.'

Me: 'Which texts were they?'

K: 'Some early ones. About our going kayaking. I never told him because at the time I knew he would have prevented me.'

Me: 'You must delete them… or write them down on paper and save them somewhere safe. That's what I do. I have all your texts transcribed and locked away.'

K: 'I should have, I know. But what the hell was he doing going through my phone messages anyway?'

Me: 'Well, maybe there is a lesson here for us. Strip both phones of messages and just make sure there is nothing untoward on them. Keep our phones safe and hidden.'

K: 'There's more. He wanted to know who "George" was, so I've had to tell him. He says he's seen you at the pool: "The tall one." He recognised you from my description.'

Me: 'Okay.'

K: 'Tim is disappointed in me. That's what it is. He feels I should have told him what I was doing and where I was going. It's his way. He thinks I've neglected the family this summer and he's especially angry at me for that.'

Me: 'Can we meet today? How about at the beach?'

K: 'No. He's home all day.'

Me: 'I'm away until Friday night.'

K: 'Shit, I'd forgotten. We'll just have to wait it out somehow. I can call you, can't I?'

Me: 'Of course, anytime. Leave a message and I'll call you back at a predesignated time. Okay?'

K: 'Yes.'

09:50

I press the end button on my phone and thump my head against the steering wheel in frustration. What the hell is this going to mean for the two of us now?

We're just going to have to be ultra-vigilant about everything – all communication, every meeting, and the way we behave in public. From here on in we will have to be so careful. I can't afford to get K into any more trouble or into any situation where she's placed under scrutiny or intense questioning at home. Who knows what this may lead to… particularly if he has a tendency to be quick with the fist.

I feel sick.

Saturday 18th September

07:40
Blue skies +18°
Back in Dorset, England.

I'm driving over to the pool but do not feel like getting in the water. I'm just hoping K will be there, so we can talk. Last night all I got was a <*x*> by text which could mean anything. I sense something is not right, something is brewing.

08:00
I'm in the water before the session starts but my head is a ball of cotton wool; maybe I should go and drink coffee and watch instead. But I need to see if K turns up.

I swim slowly at the back of the group, hoping the familiar, rhythmic action will clear my head. I turn onto my back and look towards the coffee bar and, shit, it's bloody Tim. He's standing ram-rod straight, staring at me! I turn back onto my front and automatically speed up as my heartbeat radically increases. What the heck is going on? He's never been to watch before. It must mean K is here, surely?

08:10
The main set is about to start when a familiar shape slips into the water a few metres down the pool. She's not smiling. Her face is drawn and there's barely a change of expression when I catch her eye. Aware that Tim is watching, I don't get too close to K; instead we behave like keen club swimmers and follow the instructions of the coach to the letter.

08:30

This is far from enjoyable and it's stressful. Tim is still standing at the window looking down on us. There's been no opportunity to say anything to K. And on top of that my swimming technique is dreadful. The others are asking whether I am okay or if I'm ill.

08:58

The session is almost finished, and I float about in the shallow end. K clearly has a lot of frustration to burn off and is still swimming untiringly up and down the pool. I slowly climb out. At least we can talk outside the changing rooms. K sees what I am doing and exits the pool quickly behind me.

'It's been a nightmare,' she says. 'Can you meet later? I've got to take Anna to ballet, and we can chat briefly there. I have a letter for you, too.'

'Yes, I can.'

She hurries into the changing room. This is a K I've not seen before and I'm unnerved. She's not smiling – K always smiles – and looks leaner in the face. Her bright blue eyes are dulled. What has been going on while I've been away?

11:15

Anna and K are inside the dance hall, where I can hear the piano and the barked staccato counts of the instructor. I've sent a text to K telling her I am going to go and sit in my car. It's raining for the first time in months; the kind of half-baked drizzle that Scots call mizzle and I call plain annoying. Surely summer can't be over already? I'm still in my shorts and flip-flops and hope to remain so until at least November.

K sticks her head around the door, and I flash my headlights to signal where I am. She looks up at the skies, pulls a face, and then runs over. She breaks into a smile as she approaches and hops in quickly.

Behind the obscurity of steamed-up windows, I throw my arm around her and we kiss, her wet hair rubbing against my face. My God, it's good to have her back invading my space. Like the VU metre on an Akai tape machine, the needle goes straight to the red and stays there as long as K remains in my company. Leave, and the needle drops to zero as the world goes silent.

'You have a letter for me?'

'Yes, here it is, but read it later, there isn't time now. I've missed you so much. It's been horrible. Things are all changing.'

'How?'

'He's clamping down on everything and doesn't want me to do anything without him being involved.'

'What!'

'I have to be the housewife. That's what I signed up for. And that's what I must return to.'

'But-'

'Don't worry, we will still see each other, I can't survive without seeing you, we will find a way to be together, even if it means being… I don't know what.

'I have to go. He's on my case all the time and I said I would… Anyway, I'll call you later. He's working late tonight.'

'Please make sure you do.'

'Hey…'

'What?'

'Nothing.'

'Okay.'

18:30
Back home and on my sofa.

Wednesday
(Rain – bloody everywhere!)

22,

What the frig am I doing? Fast losing grip on reality and all my common sense has finally deserted me. We could sell the rights to this film you know.

A small-town housewife and mother of three swims and kayaks with the man of her dreams and decides to ignore her family while pursuing the life of Riley with the aforementioned Odysseus (same body but perhaps unfortunately, not yet married to Penelope). All I need to do now is write the ending. The final chapter!

Now a reality check. This is how I see it:

Option 1:

We endure the current situation, meeting only occasionally to not quite quench the thirst but suffering the torture of absence and wilful deceit of others at all other times.

Option 2:

You fall in love with someone else and leave me bereft for a (long long) while, knowing it's for the best.

Option 3:

Tim discovers the real depth of our relationship and it's all over (but for whom?)

Option 4:

No further contact until predetermined future date. Both turn up on our secret bathing ledges and then leave together, forever.

Option 5:

Do a Reggie Perrin (but I'd miss the kids!)

Option 6:

TBA!

No heroics as a result of these mean words please. Despite the inconvenience of having such strong feelings, what we have is so very, very special, which is why I'm being very badly selfish and carry so much guilt. But think of it this way: even if transient and undiscovered, what memories we'll have to carry into our dotage!

I love you so.

44 x

PS. 'It is very unnerving to be proven wrong, particularly when you are really right and the person who is really wrong is the one who is proving you wrong and proving himself, wrongly, right. Right?' (The Reptile Room.)

PPS. But, why, oh why, doesn't it feel the same?

18:35

Oh shit. Time for a serious consultation with myself.

Sunday 19th September

07:00
F4-5 SW, rain +14°

I've read K's letter repeatedly and am feeling despondent and sullen. Life isn't always fair, but sometimes you have to look at it in the face and act in the best interests of the many rather than the few.

I have a horrible feeling that something along the lines of Option 4 may be required.

The way I see it,

Tim and K have become complacent and have little in the way of a real connection anymore. Only the children are keeping things alive. K needs time and space to get her home life and marriage back on track without the distraction of me. If they were to take greater care of one another, why would she ever want to spend time with me?

She should be given time with him (and away from me) to try to re-ignite their relationship. Isn't this the fairest thing to do?

Then, after a period of time, and however long we agree to be apart, she can decide whether she wishes to remain with Tim or be with me – somehow.

And I should put more effort into my relationship with Lois.

Surely, this is the most sensible thing we can do?

Monday 20th September

16:00
F4-5 S, rain +15°

Not heard anything from K today at all. No texts or calls, nothing. I hope she will be at swimming tonight.

19:15
I'm in the water but there is no sign of K. Where is she?

Tuesday 21st September

08:45

The phone is ringing; it's K at last!

Me: 'Are you okay?'

K: 'No. No I'm bloody not.'

Me: 'What's the matter?'

K: 'He's stopping me from swimming and kayaking and all my other classes too. Absolutely everything!'

Me: 'How can he do that?'

K: (Crying.) 'We have to do everything together or as a family now. I can't get out alone anymore.'

Me: 'Oh for heaven's sake. Is he serious?'

K: 'Yes, yes, he most certainly is. I must return to the fold. To be the housewife I once was – like some sort of ridiculous nineteenth-century dutiful Amish wife.'

Me: 'Oh, no.'

Silence.

Me: 'Okay, (long pause) I've been thinking about something you said in your letter. Option 4. Maybe now is the point at which we choose to spend time apart. If we don't see each other, then it might let you get back on track with him. Understand, I really don't want to do this, but it will be a fair test. We part now and meet up in three months when you either say you want to stay with him or be with me.'

K: 'But what about you? You may have lost interest and not want to be with me?'

Silence.

Me: 'So, it will be a test for both of us.'

K: (Crying.) 'Perhaps you will want to be with Lois and… No! I couldn't bear it.'

Silence.

Me: 'What else can we do? Come up with another plan that makes sense and we can try it. This way we both give it a shot.'

K: 'Let me have a think, but nothing about it feels right.'

Me: 'No, it most certainly does not.'

Thursday 23rd September

06:45
F4-5 S, rain +15°

<What about letters, texts, phone calls if I can't see you?>

<No, I think it has to be complete silence>

07:30

<So, nothing at all?>

<Nothing>

08:50

<And we meet on our secret bathing ledges?>

<Yes, let's agree now. 2.30pm Friday 24th Dec>

11:30

<OK. If it has to be so. I will turn our phone off tomorrow. 90 days. Dec 24@2.30pm. Tomorrow will be the last time and then into the abyss>

<To divide, is not to take away. I love you, 44>

<And I love you, 22 x>

Friday 24th September

07:00
Grey

And so, the great moratorium begins.

No good-byes (a banned word anyway) no farewells, no last-minute clandestine rendezvous – just absolute silence that is soul-rending. It is going to be some test (understatement), but it must be done. It is the only thing that makes sense right now.

My abnegation feels like abandonment, and like all cold turkey withdrawals, will be brutal in its execution.

Saturday 25th September

08:00
Grey

Miserable.

Sunday 26th September

08:00
Grey

Miserable.

SIX DAYS LATER

OCTOBER

'A simple life is all that we seek'

Saturday 2nd October

16:00
Grey

Why love, if losing hurts so much?
(C. S. Lewis)

I feel as if I've lost a vital body part. It is that shitting painful.

I've spent most of the afternoon lying on my bed replaying old voicemail messages over and over. I so love her voice.

'her voice is all a gentle song
with wings
which hover and stay–
a rhythm to listen and savour,
this all woman nightingale.'
(me)

When the words tumble from her lips, it is as if every letter has been delicately pared to remove any sharp edges. Like a skilled typesetter, she orders fonts so they please the eye and impart meaning: from Times New Roman to Gloucester Light. And I am addicted to it.

I wrap her tee-shirt around my face and deeply inhale the remnants of her scent.

'she has the fragrance
of a proper English summer
all sun and sea and greenery
and an essence of ever comfort–
that is, I'm sure just meant for me'
(me, again)

17:15

I've written an impassioned letter to K but cannot, must not, post it. We agreed. I will hold onto it and perhaps keep it for the archives.

The Proclaimers are playing on the radio:

I'm gonna be (500 miles)

Well, I would if I bloody could.

Lois keeps leaving messages checking I'm okay. I've told her I'm suffering from a bad case of food poisoning and must learn to cook properly.

'I get it,' she says.

Sunday 3rd October

16:00
Grey

Miserable and lonely and I'm lost in words.

Kiss me with words
my place is inside your palm – infinitely
nowhere else will ever do,
your right hand betwixt my left – fingers tight
it's the bustling, brimming soul of you
i want to make complicated shapes
all night
and climb inside your skin—
my place is you, under, about and in
kiss me with those words of yours
until they make me cry,
let's hold these golden moments
and never let them by
take me in your arms of comfort,
safely let me be;
chosen forever, always together
'i am not thine, i am thee'.

Windows wide open
i want to wake to the sun,
the sharpness of the light
the early morning breeze

and lie, aquiet, unbelieving—
my woman is here with me.
i seek to sense the slow release
of the night's tight entwine
and taste the longest tastes
in this plethora of thrills combined.
i wish to feel, in this nest of us
the warmth of you there
and the heat of my adjoining skin
in amidst the love worn air.
i want to wake to a ring of blue
and a smile encased with sleep
and lie sublime – for some time
to the whispering free lark
who plays the moment
in these hours of ours to keep.

Summerhugging

i
like.
to place my flesh
on yours
to feel your curves
in mine
and wrap my arms around
your frame
to hands (that do not lie)
all night,
and nestle my head in
deepest soft
to ride the flows of breathing rhyme
(untrying)

till the crimson dawn decides
to finish
the stillness of
our time.
like
i.

Kleptomania

i am compelled to say, confused,
at the ease you steal my words
before i say them.
you rip and plunder, then throw them back
to me
with so much greater shine,
all sparkly and sold;
(you – my light-fingered etymologist)
but days – when i am faster,
you let me spurn – a projectile
of words that i have graced never before,
with every letter flowing over
in taste
and essence,
so rich and fat
and full of sense;
(how do you let me do that?)

SIX DAYS LATER

Saturday 9th October

18:00
V. grey

Alone. Without. Purgatory. And *no one else* can help.

Last month K said, during a midday phone conversation, 'The morning has passed calmly with no bothersome emotional fragility, and you now have successfully fed the beast – so thank you.'

Like an addict, I need, we need, perpetual communication to retain control. I no longer know where she is throughout the day; the hourly knowledge-fix of her existence that delivers a balm unlike any other. Now I feel utterly bereft. Untethered.

I am also frightened. I know it is the same for K; she too will be suffering agonies, not able to share our story with anyone.

And to cap it all, I have no one to talk to. I require someone who will allow me to monopolise the conversation with my declarations of love for K or endless rationalisations of my disconcerting ailment. I have always been quite accustomed to my own company but have never felt so desperately alone. And living the deceit with Lois is not helping my sanity either. Urgh.

I guess I will have to try to sort this out myself. In any case our necessary secretiveness means discussing 'us' with anyone else is pointless. All I would hear is 'be cautious… think of the consequences,' etc, etc.

As K quoted in her letter, Paulo Coelho once said, 'Whenever we need to make a very important decision, it is best to trust impulse and passion because reason usually tries to remove us from our dream saying that the time is not yet right. Reason is afraid of defeat but intuition enjoys life and its challenges.'

A-fucking-men to that.

ONE MONTH LATER

NOVEMBER

'En-tan-gle-d
You, your lovingness... just too much'

Monday 15th November

08:20
Brightening, +15°

Hah! K has succumbed to temptation.

A letter has arrived!

(Alone at work)

22,

I miss you.

I miss your letters. I miss you. I miss being curled up with you somewhere listening to you read the words aloud – words that would sometimes put cracks in your voice. I miss your handwriting and reading your thoughts. I miss rereading your letters over and over whenever you're absent. I often miss you. I miss you as often as I miss reading your letters.

'I've tried to close the book
but the past slides out of its leaves to haunt me,
and it seems wherever I look,
phantoms of irreclaimable happiness taunt me.'
(A. E. Housman)

Today, Friday November 12th, the blunting of emotion at work, the pushing down of what has been threatening to block my throat lasted until I got into the car to drive home. What was in my throat poured out of my eyes. I have pushed it away again temporarily but it all needs to come out. I need to let go and cry so badly, but do not want the children to see. I wonder how you are doing. Is work a distraction or are equivalent feelings distracting you from it?

I wish I could speak to you again. Text even. But our phone has remained untouched in my drawer at work alongside your letters and cards, the few photos of you, my blue birthday boat and the special wooden box. Can't bear to look at any of it and won't. I expect you've taken down all the bits of me in your office for similar reasons.

I hope to catch sight of you at the pool from afar or out somewhere – so that I don't wither and die. Well, I'm bound to wither further but with the right form of training, my heart may learn to bear the strain. (Note: may?)

BUT… what if I have an uncontrollable urge to drive in a westerly direction towards your house… what if you or I can't take it anymore? What if… (are you really that strong?)

I will try my best to do my duty for the sake of the children but what use is a deadened heart? The rest means nothing if you are not truly happy etc, etc. People stay alive for the sake of relationships, and good ones, few and far between, are worth sacrificing a few material goods for. I now know this.

I could ramble on but haven't got the energy or will to write anything profound or moving. Empty. Big hole where my heart used to be. Where's it gone? Greenground. That little house with lots of light and good views.

I love you so.

44 x

PS. Did you catch sight of the stars last night?

PPS. Sorry for writing and breaking our agreement.

PPPS. Have you tried holding one hand inside the other, right palm over left knuckle? It feels like your hand is in mine.

PPPPS. I can't picture your face anymore. Help!

Bollocks to this. I'm going to post my letter, then.

'Greenground',
Bere Regis
Dorset
Monday 15th Nov 2004

44,

There is very little bravery in doing what I felt I had to do. Seeing your face and your eyes showed me the strain and worry that I have been putting you under. I can't do that to you. It is not fair. I believe that you owe it to Tim to try to be the person he married all those years ago. You can't attempt to give, if one's head is permanently elsewhere... and that is just not right. You must give it a go and give what the two of you and your children require. If then, after the efforts the two of you have made, it simply isn't working and it is still a life of mediocrity, a life of two distant partners under one roof, upsetting your family, then that is the time to consider... other things (me!)

I am here for you, you must know that. I am trying with Lois but... it's... just not the same. What we have wanted at all times is entwinement (or should that be entwine-meant?) to stay connected at all moments and be connected at all moments, only then do we feel sated. Apart and without one another the grief of separation is unbearable. As leg buckling as it is when we see each other and entwine after minutes/hours/days/weeks (!) of separation, the reverse is true for all the wrong reasons when we are apart. My legs buckle – not as a result of the euphoria of our touch and combined-ness but because of the despair and pain of being apart. I am convinced we are the same soul divided into two. It explains so much and why this pain is so disabling and can only be relieved when we are entwined.

I love you, only you and I know I will not find a more complete person to be with, for what we have is such a great and special thing. A higher love. And hearts and parts do not come along like this that often. You know this.

Like you, I can't write much more. It comes in fits and starts and if I think of you too much it brings on that condition that starts in my chest, stops me breathing and makes me want to sit down and put my head in my hands... before tears form (usually failing). I must admit, a good cry does make one feel temporarily relieved... until things I see remind me of you and us together and some of the simple and pleasurable things we have done.

It's just as well, I'm so incredibly tough to cope with all of this (a big not!).

PS. You know 'Your touch is such a painless tattoo of places forever summer.'

I wrote this for us – You+Me, 44+22 (2424):

blissful fit

our bodies fit, as pieces fit,
like snowflakes on the ground,
and our fingers fit like our bodies fit
on slow walks along the shell-lined shore;
your hip sits neatly into mine
and the pit of my arm plays shelter
to your shoulder;
our noses nestle upon each other,
and eyes they fail to blink,

our feet – like ducks, play herringbone
(so neat)
and back-to-back we fit the same
like a mirror set for one.
but, your lips they fit—
of course they do,
and as i lie alone
and scour my mind
i seek – just one misfit;
(for how much easier then—
it would be
to love you,
one
little
piece
less).
22 x

PPS. Enclosed are a few photos. You, your blue boat and watery places where we have been together. Special places. Keep them safe and secure – away from any intruder's grubby mitts.

PPPS. You are that layer beneath my tee, that floating space which never leaves.

TWO DAYS LATER

Wednesday 17th November

09:30
The postman has delivered two more envelopes. Thank Christ!

Inside the first is a card featuring G. L. Brockhurst's masterpiece 'Dorette' (1932) – the misery – and inside K has copied out a poem by Jami:

I shall roll up the carpet of life when I see
Thy dear face again, and shall cease to be,
For self will be lost in that rapture, and all
The threads of my thought from my hand will fall;
Not me wilt thou find, for this self will have fled:
Thou wilt be my soul in mine own soul's stead.
All thought of self will be swept from my mind,
And thee, only thee, in my place shall I find;
More precious than heaven, than earth more dear,
Myself were forgotten if thou wert near.

The second envelope is a letter and it has me in bits.

Tuesday
Another day at work (in body)

22,

For a woman in the medical trade to be so obviously 'on the edge' and occasionally 'over the edge' is not a good thing. My colleagues say I look tired and when I am asked if I am okay my tears involuntary well up. I cry, for my eyes are the words of a play – a tragedy about the course of true love that can be read by anyone who witnesses them.

Have you been crying too? My tears are far too big for my eyes and so they fall… endlessly fall. I have a lot of crying to do. Releasing the enormous stress and guilt of recent months and mourning the loss of something very special. Is it so fragile to slip away into a catalogue of memory? After so short a time, denied the chance to really know each other. The odds are against the dream becoming a reality, I fear. Eyes are now pink and very small.

Struggling through my day, I often wonder how you are. I think you are taking this too far. A gentle letdown would have been easier. To wean ourselves by cutting down the texts and the phone calls first. Perlease! This way is too cruel and I don't think it will help me do my best at home. I'm actually as miserable as sin, and on the very top of the list of priorities seems to be to find out if you are alright. I will the phone to ring, or see the magical promise of 'new message received'. I don't suppose those three words will ever bring me the same thrill. It was always you, immediate and reassuring. I have saved only fourteen of your text messages and all of them reflect the feelings of complete desperation I have now. I would send all of them back to you verbatim, from me, if I could.

'I who swim
In the stealth of a dream
Listening to the mind's insane silence scream.'
(Solomon Deressa)

But of course that's not what all this is about, is it? It's about me falling in love with my husband again. And for you to be 'free' of the emotional cord that binds you to me (who is not free). We try to dress it up in different terms. To continue in a marriage where things are okay, until a point where the children are grown; you have enough financial security to accommodate a partner with baggage and/or Mr G intervenes and decides we've suffered enough; or more likely, you tell me you've found love with Lois or with someone else who fits the bill and is single. Because now you know what you're looking for it will be easier. (It's easy for me to say anyway.)

But how can I comply? No paddling? No swimming? These are things that are always inside us, which are in fact us – and so cannot be taken or pushed away. 'And to be alive is very wonderful when, at last, one is.' But to live as I am at the moment is utterly wretched. I am not alone – but I am so lonely.

Yester(family)day, at Worbarrow Bay: My children's sunny smiling faces and with eyes that sparkle as they played by the sea, as a profound sadness slowly overwhelmed me and I cried. I have no clear vision of a future anymore, just lots of uncertainty and an unmoveable fear.

At home a little later (and nearly bedtime)

It is so quiet here now. The children are asleep.

Tim's on some training course somewhere (thank goodness he's not here to witness the state I'm in) and where are you? I wish you were outside my house. I've walked to the end of the road to check, but no, the street is deserted. 'Except for the street be full of stars.' But what keeps me awake is conjuring new ways to be Alive again with you. 'You-I' moments, hours, days, weeks… and the realisation that snatched seconds, disguised as hours, without… (and here I would see the interlacing of our hands on this page, numbers 22 and 44 locked together) is just not enough… does not satisfy the thirst.

'I lie within the orbit of your parting and returning breath.' (Breytenbach) I know I'm rambling; I'm tired and it's late and there is so much I still want to say.

I was reading the children their bedtime story earlier and came across this, from Willoughby:

Willa was tired, so Willa went to bed.

'And when the morning wakes me up, will you still be here?' asked Willa.

'Of course. I'll still be here,' said Willoughby.

'Good,' said Willa. 'That's the happiest thing of all!'

'Goodnight, Willa,' said Willoughby.

But Willa didn't answer.

Willa was already sound asleep.

Happy ever after?

I love you.
44 x

PS. In case you had forgotten, these are some of the things I like: loose leaf tea, shops with brown paper bags, vegetables from the garden, getting up early, hot baths, ticking clocks, firelight, sleeping with the window open, being on my own sometimes, extraordinary trees, big sky, high places, watery places, the colour blue, the smell of old roses, sweet peas, blue rain, beautiful writing, libraries, old books, big words, getting lost in the garden, English apples, fresh figs, a good film, a glass of wine, holding hands and my true love's breath.

PPS. I often dream of sleeping under the stars with the sound of the waves in my ears, trusty boat by my side – but my eyes are always open! Do you dream with your eyes open too? It's the only way.

10:15

I cannot do this to her, to us, anymore. I HAVE to see her.

Tomorrow, somehow, somewhere, I'll intercept and surprise her. I must.

Stuff this bloody agreement.

Thursday 18th November

14:45
V. wet +6°

It's raining cats and dogs and every other sort of animal too, making driving to where I believe K will be (at one of two possible workplaces) unnerving. How ironic if I should run off the road now. I am going to tell her that I cannot live without her in my life. I, we, cannot continue with this separation business any longer. It has been the most painful experience of my life and this from someone who has had several knee operations in their time. Death of the heart being the very worst death of them all.

15:00
I can see her car, so I know she's here. All I have to do now is wait for her to leave the building. I'm wearing a raincoat and a cap with a scarf wrapped around the lower part of my face, and I wonder if she'll recognise me. She's only ever seen me in shorts and tee-shirt (or nothing at all, I think stupidly).

15:30
There she is now, and already adrenalin is flooding my system. She's walking quickly with a magazine held over her head, which is already sodden. I stay out of sight by moving around the tree trunk as she approaches, waiting until she has drawn level before I start to walk beside her.

Her head is tilted down trying to avoid the pooling water.

She suddenly becomes aware and lifts her head in curiosity. I smile and we both stand still. K's jaw almost falls to the floor before rebounding from the mirror-wet paving. I step closer and look into her eyes as we say – *absolutely nothing.* Then in perfect unison, we turn and walk side by side towards her car.

Finally, K turns and says, 'You've come back for me?'

'Yes, I have, sweetheart. I have come back for you.'

I hold open my arms and she falls effortlessly into them, just as before.

'I can never leave you,' I say.

'Thank you,' she says. 'Thank you, oh, thank you.'

15:50
We agree to turn back on all the channels of communication and rip up the stupid no-contact deal. We will meet tomorrow afternoon at my house. Oh, yes!

22:55
K's bedtime text:

> *<My lion, if I should ever get back home under our double star you will cry at the sight of the wounds I have sustained in my struggle to keep my soul whole>*

Friday 19th November

06:35
Not raining anymore! +10°
Life forecast: Back on track ↑

It's remarkably sunny today!
Sent K a text on my way out this morning, hoping she'd receive it the very moment our phone went back on.

> *<I remember how to smile again. It's easier this way>*

11:40
Multiple texts from K so far.

> *<You took my breath away (again)>*
> *<Contact with you is my lifeblood. Pls don't stop... being imparadis'd is the killer>*
> *<All lose, whole find>*
> *<They who keep one another Alive, ne'er parted be>*

I reply.

> *<The heart has its reasons which reason knows nothing>*
> *<There are no shortcuts to anywhere worth going>*
> *<You know, I have left the front door of my house open every night in the hope that you may walk in>*

17:40

K is on her way over now. It may only be for a short while but were it to last for only two minutes, I'd be happy.

18:00

may i feel said he
(i'll squeal said she
just once said he)
it's fun said she
(may i touch said he
how much said she
a lot said he)
why not said she
(let's go said he
not too far said she
what's too far said he
where you are said she)
may i stay said he
(which way said she
like this said he
if you kiss said she
may i move said he
it is love said she)
if you're willing said he
(but you're killing said she
but it's life said he
but your girl said she
now said he)
now said she
(tiptop said he
don't stop said she

oh no said he)
go slow, said she
(cccome? said he
ummm said she
you're divine! said he
(you are Mine said she)

20:00

Indeed, and thank you Mr Cummings. I could not have expressed the last two hours of my life any better. Erubescence rules!

20:40

A text from K and it's a bit naughty.

<I wear you>

Saturday 20th November

12:00
Not raining anymore! +14°
Life forecast: ↑
Exercise outlook: ↑

Deep in the afterglow. I feel as if I have been released from St Helena. My colour vision has returned, and I wish to re-join the world. Jokes are suddenly funny, unprovoked irritation at everything and everyone has evaporated, my permanently furrowed brow has lightened and I feel years younger!

At swim training today I overheard someone say, 'Crikey, he's going well – again.' What a nice word is 'again', so much better than 'before'. It felt effortless in the water, as effortless as being with K. My effortless woman, which should be a hoisted neon sign whenever I'm in the vicinity of number 44.

But K's ban on swimming is still in place.

People are asking where she is. I shrug my shoulders, shake my head and look as quizzical and disappointed as they are.

12:30
Seeing K again yesterday was like re-railing a stricken locomotive. We are off once again, steaming joyfully through the countryside, and this time the brakes are not going to be applied at any time soon.

But our immediate concern is how and when we can see each other.

If K is to be forbidden from the swimming club or not be allowed out on the water, then the only opportunity for us to meet is by ducking and diving around her daily work and school run routines. It's far from ideal.

TEN DAYS LATER

DECEMBER

'There is so much we could do together... if we were together'

Monday 6th December

09:40
Cool +7°
Life forecast: ↑
Exercise outlook: ↑

My kind postman has delivered a smart light blue envelope.

Sunday
(Supposed to be gardening)

22,

There is so much we could do together, if we were together, which we're not. I have to keep reminding myself of this because it's so easy to forget. I'm struggling more and more with my 'double life', and perhaps we need to be brutal again unless we can justify my despicable behaviour somehow. Trouble is not being feline; I'm fast running out of lives, having already died a number of times.

You know how we feel 'stuck'. Because a satisfactory solution has not been found, because you do not want to break up a family and I wouldn't otherwise leave my current situation and know it is within my power to make my marriage work (if it's to be, it's up to me). Why bother? If I can give another (with effort) what I give to you effortlessly, and if you can do the same, then pukka! Having then settled back into a 'nice' comfortable life, alive but not Alive, selflessly attending to other people's happiness, we can commend ourselves on such noble deeds and only wonder what life may have otherwise been, had we chosen selfishness over piety.

But I still find myself daydreaming about what might be. Then the reality of my position wakes me up, sharply. The children will always be part of me and they have not been part of 'us' etc. etc.

In my mind the alternatives are: being honest with Tim and allowing him the opportunity to find fantastic love (it does exist!); ceasing to see you until next summer (and the way I react to separation, I'll be a white-haired old lady by then!) or trying out life on my own with the children. I have found myself looking through estate agent windows and imagining the simple, frugal life I would (have to) live. I know Tim has too, but we haven't really tackled it head-on yet.

Things at home are settled and polite. We are both doing our best, being our best and it's okay. But because it's okay, I feel terribly guilty. After all, trust is the bedrock of marriage, or any significant relationship. I am (usually) a trustworthy person. Although I don't tell untruths, the bits I leave out are parts of a bigger lie.

But… and it's a big but… if you read this and decide once again that you need to save me from myself, my grief will be so great, so profoundly great that the options we talked about in September, notably Option 1: Endure current situation, meeting only occasionally to not quite quench the thirst but suffering the torture and deceit at all other times, and Option 3: Tim discovers us and it's all over (but for whom?) would become a dead cert. So, we need to talk and talk and talk until everything is sorted between us. If we are going to cut our own shadow (read that Oscar Wilde story I gave you – please) let's do it with a ceremony and have some solid plans.

'If you spend your time trying to figure out what is best for you, your chores will be cautious, your decisions will take forever and your journey will be laundered in a sea of expectations.' (Milan Kundera)

I love you so.

44 x

09:55

While the past couple of weeks have been incredible, the pressures away from the moments together are mounting – as K is clearly feeling – and it is something we have to address quite soon. I'm concerned about putting K in harm's way with Tim's tendency to act heavy-handedly. Last week though, he lost his temper. Nothing to do with us, it seems – rather his general anger and frustration, so K told me. She forgot to pick up a brand of motor oil from the local DIY shop and it set him off.

'He was shouting all sorts of vile things at me, swearing in front of Anna and the boys. I managed to smuggle them up to their rooms while he stormed off into the back garden. I wish he wouldn't say such things in front of the children. I'm used to it, but they're not.'

His anger worries me – well, not me, I can fend for myself if it comes to it – but when it is directed towards K. The problem I have is I have no bloody way of finding out what he is really like to live with. I have no contact with any of K's friends or family, so my only source of information is K, and she does not like talking about it. She is married to the man and has three children by him; revealing what a complete shit he can be would be a huge embarrassment to her. But my gut feeling is that when K pampers to his ego, then everything is fine, when she fails him (as he sees it), he loses his temper and K gets it in the neck. She has also told me that he is very strict and regimented with the children (while K is much more relaxed with them) but has assured me he has never hurt them. They are 'his world' and I can appreciate that. My feeling is that he may well love K, but as an asset only.

I am also worried about something that K mentioned a few weeks ago, and then again last week. She says she has a nagging enduring pain at the top of her stomach. There is a noticeable, small, tender-to-the-touch bump. Tim has had a look and told her it's nothing, possibly a minor muscle tear, but the fact that K has mentioned it every time I've spoken to her suggests it is something that's bothering her. A muscle tear wouldn't ache through the night.

Lois has been on my case considerably of late; I think she senses something is not right between us. I have blamed work, but the fact is I find it so hard to be with her, especially when I have spent time with K. Leading a double life is not recommended and the strain and guilt is *killing me*. And now is not a good period as Christmas approaches. I feel it is time to hunker down and wait until the new year to act. Am I guilty of procrastination? Yes, I think I am, but let's keep the ship sailing on its existing heading for now and re-set the course, if that's what it takes, sometime in the new year.

Wednesday 8th December

09:40
Sunshine in parts +9°
Life forecast: ↑
Office forecast: ↑

<Think I may have persuaded him to let me back in the water!!!>

<Oh fantastic! Tomorrow night?>

<Yes!>

<Will be waiting for you @squash court #4>

<He may be taking me along though...>

<OK!!>

Thursday 9th December

18:30
Cloudy +7°
Life forecast: ↑
Exercise forecast: ↑

Lois has just called. She wants to discuss going skiing over Christmas. I've said I'll call her when I get back tonight.

18:50
Swim training.

I've deliberately arrived early to avoid the possibility of running into Tim. His car is here, so I can only presume he is inside and plans to watch her swim.

Bollocks! There he is. Standing in between the corridor to the changing rooms and the coffee bar stairs. Why the bloody hell stand there? Is he waiting for someone? For one of the children? For K? The session is about to start so it can't be her. Who is he waiting for? Me? Is there something K hasn't told me? Oh shit…

I up my pace and decide to hustle into the leisure centre like a man on a mission. I cast a glance at Tim as I pass through the swing barriers and out of habitual politeness offer him a half-smile along with a mumbled, 'Alright then?' There's no response and I'm not hanging around for any conversation. I hurry the remaining few metres to the safety of the changing room. Phew!

19:05

K's in the water chatting to the others, who have not seen her for weeks. I can see she's delighted to be back in her natural environment. I jump in behind and deliberately brush her bum.

She turns around quickly, smiling, but whispers, 'Tim…'

I nod and glance up to the viewing area and – shit, of course he's there. Face pressed to the glass, staring at us.

Right then, I say to myself, *better to pretend that K's not here and get on with this swimming lark. Look, but don't touch – and that's a shame, as the water tonight feels so much more alive now that K's back in it!*

19:59

The session is nearly finished, and I swim up casually alongside K and say, 'Changing rooms?' She gives me a single nod and a few minutes later, we meet.

'We've got a spectator tonight. Why?'

K shrugs her shoulders and looks perplexed. 'He said he'd drop me off, but I had no idea he was going to stay. I've no clue about what he's up to.'

'Perhaps he knows a bit more than we think? Have you discussed us lately?'

'No, definitely not. I've avoided all mention of sport and anything that might connect us. I genuinely don't know what's got into him.'

'Maybe your nagging about coming back to the swim club has raised his suspicions. It's got to be that, hasn't it?'

'Yeah, you're right. He probably thinks there's another reason I wanted to get back in the water. Can't think what that might be, though. Can you?'

'Hah, nope, no idea at all!'

'You free for a long chat tomorrow? We've loads to talk about.'

'Yes, definitely, give me a call anytime in the morning.'

'Okay, sweetheart, speak to you then.'

20:15

Sent K a text while I was still changing and hoped she'd read her phone before leaving.

> *<The urge to grab; so intense. To brush a fingertip along the back of your hand; a thrill. To connect fingers in palm with squeeze; a fillip. To follow your bubbles; blinding. Catching your smirk... with fervent thoughts; enlightening. To see you gone; dejection. From: Frustrated of Dorset>*

Friday 10th December

08:55
Cloudy +7°

I go to hang out my swim kit and towel to dry from last night – and what do I find? A cream envelope tucked into the corner pocket of my bag!

Thursday
(in my lunch hour)

Inamorato,

Part of me feels slightly foolish as I slip yet another envelope into your hand. But I want to remember the journey, by keeping a record of all the little pieces of heaven along the way.

I can see things differently now we are in a 'new' relationship. If either of us chooses the old life instead of the new, I won't regret a single moment in your company. You see, my thinking has changed. To bury oneself in domestics for a dozen-plus years and then suddenly look up to see the world as it was, in all its glory, unleashes many demons and shows clearly the difference between contentment and happiness – the difference between life being good and life getting much better. I now seek the latter. Acute moments of intense happiness while knowing you will be treasured and not forgotten whatever happens in the days, weeks, months, or years to come.

Each time I see you I could tell you how much I want to stay with you for the rest of the day, the rest of the night, the rest of my life. And each morning as I wake I fear the magic will slip through our fingers and be lost. I want so much to lie 'imparadis'd' every night and always have my hand in yours. If then, it all becomes ordinary and our preference is to lie towards the edge, facing away as I do most nights, contented but alone, how cruel would that be? How devastatingly disappointing.

For anything less than what we have, the stakes are too high. Even now, embedded as deeply as we are, there is a part of me that pulls back to earth, to where I am now, with what and who I know. Only because of the uncertainty of how can a love like this last. The fickle nature of emotion, the transience of feeling. Is it better, then, to keep us away from reality (as you have done before), severance to save ourselves from witnessing the death of something extraordinary? Parting in favour of the security and certainty my marriage brings? Or perhaps life is about letting go of certainties and taking a risk, in order to experience the best moments, to open life's box of treasures.

But it takes more than a touch of madness to continue as we do. We know the consequences of being discovered but common sense and reason are overpowered by the only thing that seems to matter – being with each other whenever we can. In another time and another universe, I would share your house, your bed, your life, and your name (if you would have me), because I know how to stay in love with you – always.

44 x

EIGHT DAYS LATER

Thursday 16th December

09:45
Wet F4-5 S +9°
Life forecast: ↑
Office forecast: Mixed
Exercise forecast: Good swim last night

<Have a cancelled work appointment this am, fancy company?>

<Already waiting>

Ooh! That's a bonus for a Thursday morning. K is coming over. Time for coffee then.

10:45

'I need to stroke my boat,' K says, as she walks into my kitchen. 'I'm missing my lovely blue boat. It's been ages since we last went out. When can we go out in the boats again, *please*?'

'C'mon, then, let's go and stroke your boat! If you're really lucky I'll let you stroke mine as well.'

I open up the garage door and K wanders over to her boat.

'Here we are in winter, it's dark, damp and quite miserable but this blue beauty reminds me only of our summer. Can I sit in?'

I lift the kayak off the racking and place it on the floor matting, and K drops herself in.

'Yes! I can picture us out now, paddling under those tall white chalk cliffs, listening to the noise of the waves as they fall onto the caves below…' She sighs. 'Do you think we can get out before Christmas?'

'Well, yes, as long as the weather's not too crazy, we can sneak off to the Purbeck one morning and launch from there. Let's make some plans.'

'Yes, plans, we must make plans.'

K goes to haul herself out of the cockpit, but something stops her. She winces in pain.

'Whoa! What is it?'

'Argh. This stomach muscle thing, it's getting really painful. Look, you can see it.'

K lifts her cardigan and shirt and I touch the top of her stomach. There's a small but pronounced bump just below her rib cage.

'Careful, it's so sore.'

'Really? That tender? What does Tim say it is?'

'He thinks it could be a hernia or he still thinks it's a muscle tear, but I've not been doing anything that would cause such an injury. I've not been in the gym for ages – not been allowed to!'

'Hmm. What about seeing another doctor then?'

'Yes, I think I'll see my GP. Tim is not my registered doctor. The thing is, I'm never ill, so I hardly ever go to see anyone. If this gets any worse, then I will have to. It doesn't feel like a muscle thing to me.'

We head back into the house and I make a decent pot of coffee for us both, and we retreat to the long sofa.

'Christmas is coming! What are your plans? I'm under a bit of pressure to go away.'

K's shoulders drop as she thinks about it. 'Well, I don't see myself being able to get away at all.'

'I assumed it would be tricky to meet up. It drags on for so long. There's a carol service I'd like to take you to, and, of course, we have our present swapping to arrange.'

'I'll discuss it at home, but what are your plans?'

'Lois doesn't *do* Christmas and I've never been a big fan, especially now if I can't be with you. She's badgering me about an Alpine ski trip.'

'Oh?'

'Yes, for seven days during that Christmas week then back for the new year. Nothing is booked yet, but it will all be last minute depending on the best snow, flights and so on.'

'I would so love to go skiing with you.'

'I would adore it if you could come with me sometime. That has to be at the very top of our to-do list. I cannot think of anything more romantic than being with you up in the Alps, in the high mountains, in that wonderful snow, log fires, woolly jumpers, big fluffy duvets.'

K looks at me wantonly. She's breathing deeply, her chest rising and falling, and I sense she's already got her ski kit on.

'Next year! Next year! Let's move it to the top of our wish list. Skiing in the Alps in the winter of 2005. Yes?'

'Yes! We'll make it happen!'

Friday 17th December

12:30
Clearing F2-3 N +5°
Life forecast: ↑
K forecast: Not enough

K is finishing early today as she has her work's Christmas party later, so we've decided to meet now and grab every available moment as the next ten days are going to be nigh-on impossible.

I've ordered our pot of tea for two and am sitting on our squeaky vinyl bench seat by the window, peering out at the Christmas shoppers, letting my mind wander off where it will. Here I am, it's nearly Christmas, and yet it seems only minutes ago that I was sitting opposite K in the heat of a June day – frustrated and perplexed – asking her what it was she had done to me. Where has that time gone? As K said to me once, 'Time is such a miserable commodity. When we're together there's not enough of it, and when we're not, there's too much.'

If only the clock would stop when we're together.

12:35
Stop that clock. Here she is.

K grabs my hand as she slides herself along the bench.

'I've wanted you so much today. In my mind I've been with you all morning – and all of last night!'

'I'm here now,' I say. 'And I'm all yours, despite these layers of winter clothing, I am all yours.'

'Ugh. It's just some days I feel so immersed in *us* I can't *do* anything.'

'You think you suffer alone? You drive me beyond distraction too, you know!'

'Ha-ha. Okay!'

K hands me an envelope. 'Go on, open it. This is what I did this morning – at work!'

It's a card with a photograph of a kingfisher diving into the water, and inside is K's familiar handwriting in Platinum Carbon Black Ink. The sort of ink that never fades.

'Shall I read it out loud?'

'Yes,' K says, looking around, 'but not too loud!'

Dear 22,

Hit by dysphoria. Vexed. Frangible. It whelms and whelms 'til you once again fix me with passion-filled eyes and insufflate me with your curative breath. Such presence, like too much wine, undoes me.

How I wish I were there on the floor of an upstairs room at five in the morning in front of a mirror making love with you. Two hands, complicated shapes and our entwining bodies. I want to hear your words of love over and over again melt onto my body like butter while you feed me endlessly with your kisses. If only you could rip me open and climb inside to feel the throb of your heart in mine.

You deserve to be loved like this because you share with me everything you do. I am easily lulled into sleep in your arms and taken over the brink by your touch. Only that existence will do, no other.

I love you so much.

44 x

PS. Thank you for loving me (so beautifully) x

'Whoa!' I say. 'The malaise really is bad today, isn't it! Hah. And you wrote this while at work this morning? If only your work colleagues knew what you were doing!'

'I know, they'd be so shocked.'

'The amount of time I spend thinking about you in a day, it's quite a disgrace really. If I actually calculated the hours and minutes… well, I'm amazed I achieve anything else.'

'Odd you should mention that. I was looking at my mobile phone history last night and do you know how many hours we have talked on our phone? Have a guess.'

'Seventy-five hours?'

'Get outta here.'

'One hundred and fifty…?'

'That's more like it… but more.'

'Two hundred!'

'The actual hours since July is two hundred and sixteen.'

'But we never seem to have enough time to talk. How can it be so?'

'I know. That's what my reaction was when I worked it out. And that's me calling you. If we added your calls, it would be more. What on earth do we talk about?'

'You tell me.'

'Do you think we'll ever run out of conversation? You see couples sitting together and all they seem to talk about is such banal bollocks, nothing of importance, just trivial day-to-day irrelevant nothings. Do you think we'll end up like that?'

'We could, but I don't think so. We talk endlessly and effortlessly, and we are happy. I'll think we'll be alright. The best test way would be to try it out.'

'Yes, I agree. Next year, we'll find a solution. We'll find a way of being together.'

'Hey, come here,' I say. 'Sit on my lap.'

K slides around from the other side of the table, then places herself on my lap. She rests her head on my shoulder.

'That's better, normal service resumed,' she whispers.

The waitress appears and I ask for another pot of tea. K twists around to pick up the teapot but immediately yelps in pain loud enough to frighten both the waitress and me.

'What? Is that your tummy thing hurting?'

'Oh, God, yes,' K groans.

'You must see your doctor straight away. You can't mess about if the pain is persisting.'

'It's on my list to do this afternoon. I've got to know what it is.'

'Yes, and let me know what they say.'

THREE WEEKS LATER

A NEW YEAR

JANUARY 2005

'I hope you are as happy as you can be'

Monday 10th January

20:31
Biting NE, F4-5, cloudy, -2°

Returned from foreign travels.

K sent me a strange text message while I was abroad with Lois. The moment I read it I knew something wasn't right. Not her usual style and so much out of character, calling me by my name(!) and using the dread-inducing words, 'I hope'. The text was also sent in the early hours of Sunday morning.

<Seacombe. I hope you are as happy as you can be. 44 x>

20:40
And then. When I open up my computer at home, I read this email.

To: Seacombe <geobar22@hotmail.co.uk>
From: Katherine King<kk44@hotmail.co.uk>
Subject: Our world

'All the long sad nights, and all the strong
and sensible vows. And now he had come
And there she stood.'
(Dorothy Parker)

Mi Amore,

My world has shrunk to a handful of people who really matter. I have ached for you more this week than ever before.

On my desk is a collection of cards from people who care about me. Everyone cries as soon as they see me, and I have cried with them and had more hugs in one week than I can ever remember. You see, I have cancer… and they think it could be really bad.

As I sit here, I immediately wonder how you will cope. This is a real tragedy of the highest order and yet… and yet it could be a solution to our problem if Tim agrees. I have now told him about us. I have told him I love you – unequivocally and that a life with you, by your side is what I desire and need. We will talk to the children.

This is certainly not the solution we wanted, but it is an answer. This thing has been hiding deep inside my tummy and my worry is that you will abandon me when you see I'm not healthy. I have made a promise to myself that I will be fitter and healthier than I have ever been and I certainly have the motivation (you!) – but I can't do it without you. I may become weak and terribly unwell, which I know you don't cope well with. If it's any consolation, neither do I.

When I stepped into the consultant's room at Bournemouth Hospital to hear the news I didn't want and couldn't believe, I felt sick and wanted to run away and put all my gear on. I'm a swimmer, I run, I keep fit and healthy, have well-worn walking boots, a blue boat, a paddle and lots and lots of clothes that make me feel like the person I believe myself to be. I do not belong in hospital. As I write, the fear returns and my pulse starts racing.

The only way I can get through this is if you are alongside me. I don't go anywhere without my wooden box and Viktor Frankl's book, but if you leave me, I'm dead and for once I'm not exaggerating.

You may be surprised when I tell you something good, something wonderful may come from this and I feel very fortunate to have been given the chance to see the world through a fresh pair of eyes (I ordered blue again). I had been incredibly low since before Christmas and felt completely stuck, as you did. Life was far too stressful to enjoy, and I wasn't as nice to live with as I should have been – because I couldn't have what I wanted and even when you said I could, it wouldn't come quickly enough. I now know exactly what is important in life and what is not. People matter, nothing else. It is relationships with people that make us happy and allow us to grow – the right ones in particular! I am grateful for what each day brings – sounds crass but it is true. These things change us for the better and I hope I can teach you more about yourself and how to be happy through this experience, which will humble us both, I'm sure.

Let's enjoy life to the full together while we can. We can do anything now, as long as we're not hurting anyone else. How liberating is that! I want to spend as much time with you as I can and with the children so you can get to know me as I am with them – Mary Poppins in action! When they are at school, I can share your space and let you work but be there too. We can train together as long as I am well, and when I'm not you can have another life until I'm better again and able to challenge you on and in the water. I'm sure I'll have enough insurance money for us both to go to all those places we dream about, do all the things we want to do. This is our opportunity – will you agree to grasp it? Live for the f-ing moment with me. Please!

Once I know exactly what we're dealing with and how and when 'they' are going to treat it – we'll put our diaries together. Won't we?

I can stay in my high tower and we will love each other forever and ever and everyone can know it. No one can take this from us now and we can finally live for the moment – because this moment is all there is.

I cling to Tim like a drowning woman to a rock – but he cannot keep me alive. Only you can do that.

I love you, my soldier.

44 x

I am… in pieces and I feel… *destroyed.*

In absolute shock, I tap out a reply – of sorts.

To: Katherine King<kk44@hotmail.co.uk>
From: Seacombe <geobar22@hotmail.co.uk>
Subject: Our world

Oh Sweetheart,

That weird text from you the other night, then no communication at all, my strange painful stomach cramps and then an overwhelming feeling of gloom. I sensed it was something serious, and something larger and more threatening than we have had to deal with hitherto. How many more frigging tears do we have to shed? Tears normally occasioned because of our separation and the impossibility of our situation.

However black it may appear though, we can fight it. We can. We are used to tough news and have always managed to battle our way through, and we can do it again. It can be done; it can, because you are exceptional. You are exceptional in everything you do. You are an exceptional person (and I love you). You have the mental focus to conquer this. It exists within you and must be channelled to fight this cancer.

You need to become selfish, very selfish – demand what you need.

Remember. I remain by your side – always.

I love you & beyond—

x

PS. We can beat this x

Tuesday 11th January

09:00
Bitter NE -2°
Life forecast: ←→Has been better
Exercise outlook: Will swim or will go mad

After the news yesterday, I thought I was going to be up all night but, surprisingly, I slept soundly. Perhaps it's the travel catching up with me, or maybe the belief that out of this new catastrophe there is a possibility that we can be together… forever.

With my morning pint of tea in my hand, I'm slowly coming to terms with the new reality and the scale of the mountain to be conquered. The tasks in front of us are enormous, and if I am to have any chance of reaching the summit with K by my side, then I need a clear-cut plan. And I don't believe I have any time to waste.

Righto.

Number 1. I have to talk to Lois. I have to tell her – admit to her – that I'm sorry, but I have been a COMPLETE BASTARD! Yes, I have been spending time with another woman and I've fallen in love with her. I can't be with her… but I am in love with her. And I'm so sorry for not telling you sooner.

Number 2. I need to tell my family about K; who she is and what she means to me, and what the current situation is – we are going to need their support. Need to advise Graham.

Number 3. Talk to a solicitor and take advice about divorce. How bumpy is the process going to be?

Number 4. Cancer. Get on the case once we know the full diagnosis and try to get to grips with the treatment options available.

Fuck, the more I think about it, there's a bloody load of things I need to do.

Shit. Shit. Shit.

Wednesday 12th January

08:20
Grim F5-6 NE -4°

After a lot of deep breaths, I've phoned Lois and asked her to meet me later today. I said, merely, it was important.

16:00
I suspect Lois knows I'm going to suggest we separate; she's been aware I've not been myself for quite a while now. My routine excuses about work difficulties have worn thin, although she's never asked me directly about what was wrong. If she had, I would have chosen to ignore it in any case.

I feel physically sick as I draw up to the Happy Eater on the A27. Lois has already arrived and is sat at a table, brow furrowed, looking pensive. I sit opposite her and forgo any social niceties. My vision has narrowed. I feel incipient panic creeping up on me and the only thing I can do is concentrate. I force myself to tell her the truth.

'I have something to say, and I'm truly sorry.'

Lois simply stares, her jade-green eyes piercing me. I feel like I am being ripped in two.

'Last summer I met someone. Someone who has become very special to me. She's a swimmer and a kayaker. And, well, I'm in love with her.'

Lois's face tightens and there is a blaze of anger in her eyes. 'I bloody knew it. I *knew* you were seeing someone else.'

'I'm sorry, it just happened, and I know I should have told you sooner, but everything about it was, is, too difficult.'

'Trust and commitment have always been super *difficult* for you, you shit.'

'Something else has happened, too, and it's complicated things even more.'

'What? The cow is about to calve?'

'No, not unless it is a re-run of the Immaculate Conception. It's not that. She has been diagnosed with a type of stomach cancer and they think it could be really bad.'

'Oh, okay. I'm sorry, that's terrible. Poor woman. What's her name?'

'Katherine. She's married with three young children.'

'Hah. What a mess.'

'I love her – and about which I can do nothing. Nobody planned for it to happen. It just did.'

'And she loves you, presumably?'

'Yes, yes, she does.'

Lois's face is starting to go red – past experience tells me she's about to blow. I sit back in my chair and prepare myself.

'Well, good luck with it all. I wish her well, I truly do, but as for you…'

Lois stands and jabs a finger in my face.

'*You* can royally fuck off. I never want to hear from you again, ever. Got it? You lying piece of pusillanimous shit.'

She walks out with her head held high, but I can see she's crying. I feel as low, as abject, as I ever have in my entire life. Lois deserves better.

Thursday 13th January

07:15
Thermals x 5, NE cold -1°

It's K calling on the house phone.

K: (In tears.) 'It's not good news at all.'

Me: 'Oh shit.'

K: (Crying noisily.) 'That's what I said.'

Me: 'Tell me.'

K: 'The MRI scan has revealed I have a metastatic pancreatic tumour and it is non-operable. I've also a secondary tumour in my backside. The oncologist and my consultant have both recommended a course of chemotherapy ASAP – for twelve weeks, with something called gemcitabine. I will be monitored regularly and have scans every two weeks. They say this is the best option for me.'

Me: 'Right. What does all this mean? I'm confused.'

K: 'I'll explain when I see you. There is some good news though.'

Me: 'Really? What?'

K: 'Tim has said I can come and stay with you next week if I want to!'

Me: 'Wow!'

K: 'Yes. I've told him I have to be there with you! That's it, that's all I said.'

Me: 'Did he get angry?'

K: 'No, not at all. He was very solemn. Impassive almost. I can't get *any* reaction out of him.'

Me: 'Hmm. How is your level of pain? Has it got any worse?'

K: 'It's there all the time. They have given me painkillers, but they're beginning to make me feel a bit strange.'

Me: 'I can imagine.'

K: 'Anyway, I'm going to swim tonight, so I'll see you there – and then I'll be over for the weekend and next week! Did you speak with Lois?'

Me: 'Yes, yes, I have. She knows about us now.'

K: 'Okay.'

Silence.

Me: 'See you in the water later. I love you.'

K: 'I love you too.'

I put the phone down and crawl back upstairs to my bed and drag the duvet over my head. It's safer under here. What the bloody hell is going on? It's all happening so damn fast and I don't know if I'm ready. But how can anyone be prepared for this sort of situation? I'm just going to have to tackle it full on; stick some armour plating on and get on with it. Take each battle as it comes. The goal is worth it, of course…

I need to speak with K about Tim, though. What exactly is going on inside his head?

09:15

Internet research.

My mood has slumped.

She doesn't do anything by halves, this woman. She really could have chosen so many other parts of the body to get this stinking disease. It appears cancer of the pancreas is one difficult so-and-so. The web is crammed full of information, research data, statistics, true-life stories, treatments, the causes – it goes on and on, but the recovery stats don't look good? Why not? I don't understand.

Clearly, I need to bone up on everything pertinent – I only have a rather average grade 'C' in A level biology to fall back on, and this stuff is – well, a bit of a minefield.

21:15

Swam this evening and K was there in the top lane, just as she said she would be. Determined not to let anything stop her from doing what she absolutely loves.

There are a few rumours going around that K is unwell, and a number of club members had brought cards and get-well notes. It was quite an emotional thing to see friends being so warm and sympathetic, but I was also surprised at how fast news travels.

No one mentioned *us* as a pairing – a bit too sensitive a subject at this stage, or perhaps the majority are unaware – but I stood next to K throughout and was very much part of the conversations afterwards.

One thing at a time. I'm sure the word will go around once we allow it.

Saturday 15th January

10:31
Grey, F1-2 cold +5°
Life forecast: ⟷
Exercise outlook: ⟷

I've tried writing a number of emails. After months of clandestine meetings, and without a whisper to anyone, I'm drafting missives that try to explain to family and friends who K is and what has been really going on in my life! Describing the complexities of our relationship without it sounding like a Barbara Cartland novel isn't easy.

Got as far as the first page for my mum and my dad, uncle and aunt, two brothers and a few old school friends, but gave up in frustration at the size of the task.

All I know is that the toughest battles are saved for the strongest soldiers and I believe K is one strong soldier.

15:05
Started to bookmark a number of websites about pancreatic cancer. Have found some historic case reports and a charity offering some information, but very little from any national authority, read – nil! So much of the information is for those based outside of the UK and is full of dubious scientific jargon or American spiritual woo.

Do only Americans get this wretched disease?

17:30

<All OK for tomorrow?>

<Yes, all OK, children heading off to parents will be over late afternoon>

<From owl till lark>

Sunday 16th January

10:31
Snowdrops out, cold, +3°
Life forecast: ↓ ↑ ↓ ↑
Tulips & chimneys: ↑
Exercise outlook: ↑

19:00
Supper is keeping warm under the grill and will be ready soon. I've set the table for two, lit the fire, candles in place, made the bed, everything is prepared.

Just need *my woman*.

20:00
We're lying on the sofa in front of the fire and the only light is coming from the burning logs. Shadows perform their jittery mime on the walls and ceiling and are as mesmerising as watching the thunderous, storm-powered waves that crash and explode onto our secret limestone bathing ledges.

'You know there's nothing to hold us back now? You can throw away that medal you've been wearing with so much gallantry. We can be together – finally.'

'You think so?' I say.

'Yes, the moment is here for numbers twenty-two and forty-four to be together as 2424 properly. It's here. We can do it. No need to hold back now; we're hurting no one. The hurt is done. We're allowed this. We can finally, finally, be together – properly.'

I lift myself onto my elbow and we face each other. Smiling, but deeply nervous inside like a virgin teenager, I begin to undo the buttons of K's cardigan, then remove it from her shoulders. She pulls the zip down on my jumper and lifts it over my head. Slowly, we reduce the layers, one by one, all the way down to soft, silky black lace and hugging cotton over our winter-white flesh. I unclip K's bra and let it fall down between us, and watch how the flickering flames dance upon the contours of her breasts. K runs her nails down my back, and I feel a tingle shoot through my body. I bite her lip and hang onto it, then nibble her tongue before kissing her passionately – intimately – as we always do, before falling slowly backwards onto the welcoming softness of the hearthrug. I nestle my face in K's hair and inhale – memories of sea smells and big sky drench me.

Carefully, I lift up her hips and pull away the final layer, past her knees and beyond her ankles, to reveal a sacred nakedness. I kneel in front of her and let her reveal the rest of me.

'Let's go to that place,' I whisper.

'Yes,' she says simply.

I lie on my back and K straddles me. Her eyes look deeply into my being, and I watch her expression as she places her hips over mine. I enter the softest vice.

'Oh, my God. Yes!' she says with a sharp intake of breath. 'Yes,' she says, over and over again.

Her cries grow louder as our urgency increases.

Then suddenly it changes.

'No, no, no! Oh no! Please. No!'

I stop and watch as K swiftly rolls her body away from mine.

Over me, about us, on the cream-coloured rug is a pool of deepest crimson.

'Shit, shit, shit. I'm haemorrhaging. Badly. Quick, grab a towel. I must get to the bathroom.'

I lift K up into my arms and carry her up the stairs as fast as I can.

'Please, lay me in the bath,' she says, crying. 'I'm so sorry, I am frightened, I'm so sorry. My body's altering so damn fast, this is terrible. I'm so sorry, I really am.'

'I'll call for an ambulance.'

'No, no. What help can they be? Tell me I have cancer?'

'What can I do? What can I get for you?'

'Run the water, please. There is nothing to be done. I'll just let it slow. It will stop, I'm sure. It'll be fine. Let me stay in here for a little while. Please, don't worry. I'm so sorry.'

Leaving K in the bathroom, I go back into the sitting room and kneel by the fireplace. I place my head in my hands and sob uncontrollably. Curling up into a ball, I weep and weep until my stomach muscles ache.

All the control, the secretiveness, the desire, the want, the wait, and now to see so dramatically in front of my eyes that my love, my other half, is not well. My woman is not well, she is ill, is becoming really ill.

Fuck it.

Fuck it.

Fuck it.

FOUR DAYS LATER

Friday 21st January

11:31

*Brighter, +6°

With the other night quickly forgotten and after three days of round-the-clock entwinement, this morning continues to be another full of positiveness and possibilities. We draw up a list, and then another list. K goes off to find more paper and we continue with another list. All these things look positive, action-led and above all solvable.

Bizarrely as it may sound, we are both in firm agreement, that this disease could actually be the *passport* to our freedom for a new life – together. K just needs to get free of this cancer and then all other things are completely surmountable; they will just slot into place for us. Tim will not put up a battle at all after realising his relationship is beyond recoverable, the children – after seeing their mum come through such a tricky illness – will only want to see both their parent's happiness as the most crucial thing of all and will embrace this new era in their lives.

Welcome happiness, exit miserableness. Out of all this horridness will come the joy we seek and the support from close family members and others who realise that abiding love will conquer all, even if it is slightly unconventional.

16:15

<I've been told my diet has to really change. I've got to be very strict. No sugars. It's going to be so boring x>

Saturday 22nd January

18:31
F4-5, NE +1°

After a chilly paddle.

Instead of swimming this morning, K and I went out paddling in Poole Harbour. She's been nagging me for ages and today was an ideal time, although there was quite a bitter north-easterly blowing. We were dressed up like bears because of the wind chill.

We managed one lap, past Brownsea Castle and Long Island and then back in, before the wind and the tide really picked up. There is no problem with capsizing in the summer months, but in the winter, it is not recommended at all – it can be life-threatening. Actually, K was fine in the rough water; her confidence in her blue boat is really rather good.

'Thank you for today,' K said, as we reluctantly parted. 'I don't think I could ever become tired of doing this with you. Sea plus spray plus spume plus you!'

Then a short while later, I received a text; our Cummings quote and the one most appropriate for the two of us:

> *<for whatever we lose (like a you or a me) it's only ourselves we find in the sea. x>*

Sunday 23rd January

11:25
F3-4, NE +4°

K has now left Greenground to head back home and see the children and to face Tim.

I'm home alone.

Monday 24th January

08:15

To: Seacombe<geobar22@hotmail.co.uk>
From: Katherine King<kk44@hotmail.co.uk>
Subject: My husband

Writing my morning emails has become my new habit. Managing to keep in touch with so many people I seem to have ignored for years. Just like you, I am now surrounded by friends who appear regularly on my screen each day. Suits me not to have to talk or find a stamp and a post box!

With you it has been different of course. For the past eight months (exactly) I have wanted – sometimes needed – to speak to you every day and have resisted the urge to sit at my desk from morn till night writing endlessly about feelings during moments only you and I know about. Recently you have not received paper in an envelope, but that's because I have kept it all, now things have altered. Perhaps I shall show you my writings from December and January when we next get time together. A sore point.

Tim has run out of coping strategies. The days at your house last week and Saturday's paddling did it for him. He now won't let me see you! He wants me to break off with you completely! He doesn't understand how difficult – no, impossible – this would be. He only sees what he thinks would be the right thing to do, the right thing to do for him. Again, I'm thrown into a stressful situation because I will have to be creative to find the time to see you, and how can you give yourself totally to me when I only see you twice a week for just a few hours?

And I don't want to share you with someone new.

What shall we do to survive? I am at a loss to know how to manage this situation and worry about both of us and the children. Yesterday things got nasty with Tim and I got hurt (accidentally this time – honestly!) but it has made me think my priority is to keep him sweet. Today we should talk about it, in the knowledge that I don't want to live without you next to me for the rest of my life.

See you later. 1pm at the pool?

44 x

PS. I may be a few minutes late as I have to go via the health food shop and collect a hundredweight of supplements.

14:15

Swam with K, or rather played in the water with K, at lunchtime today. The pool can be quiet at odd times of the day and, fortuitously, today at lunchtime was one of those times. We had the full twenty-five-metre pool to ourselves, so naturally we reverted to being children, messing about with the kids' oversized swim floats, hoops, and rubber rings. Underwater antics and all sorts.

Then, we sat down to have a long chat. Tim, it would appear, has gone from one extreme to the other, and is now insistent on barring all communication.

'He does not want me in contact with you at all. He wants me locked into the family orbit exclusively through this illness thing. But, of course, you and I will keep on seeing each other. You are my lifeblood and I need you, despite what he says. Tim's trying to threaten me because he says I need him, and, medically speaking, I do, right now of course. Damn this bloody disease.'

'You said in your email that you got hurt. Has he assaulted you?'

'Well, it was sort of an accident, if throwing open a door into someone counts as an accident. We were arguing, and I hid myself in the bathroom. I was behind the door as he kicked it open. He wasn't to know I was standing there.'

'Did you get a bruise or a cut? Where were the children when all this was happening?'

'Just a small one, if I brush my hair back, here, you can see it.'

'Goddamn it! What was the argument about this time?'

'Something really stupid, and not directly about us.'

'What, then? Can you tell me?'

'Well, he…'

'What?'

'He wants me to *always* wear my wedding ring.'

'You had an argument about that? Surely that's crazy?'

'Well, I've not been wearing it for sport and I've kept it off all summer… and now he's really upset that I haven't been wearing it because, of course, he knows now I am in love with you.'

'He is off his rocker. I just don't believe it. Unbelievable. With everything else that is going on in your life. Surely the only focus can be on getting you better as fast as possible.'

'Yes, I think he can be *distracted* sometimes. Anyway, I'll put it back on if it pleases him, but the other problem is that I've lost it!'

'Oh, brilliant.'

'And that's why he lost his temper. He thinks something as precious as a wedding ring should never be lost. And he's right, of course, but I simply don't know what I've done with it!'

'Has he hit you at all, recently? Before yesterday?'

'Not recently, but yes, he has in the past. A fair bit. Over the years I've tried to understand what he wants from me, but somehow, I'm still letting him down. If I try really hard, I can do it, but he has standards, which I just don't seem to be able to live up to on a day-to-day level. I fail him. I don't mean to, of course, it's just that is what happens. But I do have three incredible, wonderful children, who are my world. And I have Tim to thank for them, of course.

'Look, please don't worry about this. I've lived with it long enough and can deal with it. If it should ever get truly out of hand you will be the first to know; there is no safer or better refuge than with you! Please, we have enough to worry about. I have to get better and find ways to be healthy again. You and I have so much still to do.'

'Yes, lots still to do.'

'I start my chemotherapy tomorrow, the first of twelve sessions over six weeks. I am going to need all my energy to deal with it – and will need *everyone's* support as well.'

Tuesday 25th January

09:20
Big spring tides, +2°

<The first chemo due shortly. We are all going to the hospital, the children are with me. I wish you were here with me though. I'm so very scared x>

<Dig deep, be strong x>

Thirty minutes later.

<And here I am with poison running through my veins. I'm so sad and frightened of what this pain all means. No one here seems very chirpy at all. It's very depressing x>

Wednesday 26th January

17:30

Finished an email to K, having spent a few hours researching the net.

To: Katherine King<kk44@hotmail.co.uk>
From: Seacombe<geobar22@hotmail.co.uk>
Subject: We can do this

I have been spending a great deal of time on the internet looking into the various treatments and options available to us. I must admit it is a bit of a minefield and there certainly seems to be a great deal of conflicting advice. I suspect we are going to have to look outside of the box to find the best answer. Perhaps the conventional treatment recommended by the oncologist and the consultant together with some select natural alternatives? (The best of both worlds.) I've compiled a list of remedies that have had success and maybe you want to run some of them by Tim for his opinion? Yes?

Just one thing though. Please do not spend time ploughing around the various internet sites. Leave that to me, Tim, or someone else. There's a lot of scaremongering twaddle out there.

One thing I do know though, with the right PMA (Positive Mental Attitude) and TLC we can conquer this, so you must try to stay focused all the time and not let other things distract you. It will be hard, I know, but your health is the number one priority above anyone else's needs or demands. Remember Lance Armstrong's book when he was diagnosed: 'I couldn't afford a lapse of concentration. I had to think about living, just making it through every single moment. The idea was oddly restorative; winning my life back would be the greatest victory.'

Post nubila, phoebus (after the clouds, the sun) and remember: 'Life always waits for some crisis to occur before revealing itself at its most brilliant.'

Stay strong and I love you very much.

22 x

17:45

Reading up on the internet has really quite depressed me. There is so much (mis)information out there regarding treatments for this type of cancer; some are truly wacky; others make good common sense.

And to top it all, I've just discovered that the type of chemotherapy K's currently being administered is purely palliative.

Bloody hell.

No wonder Tim allowed K to stay with me the other week. He knows all of this.

Oh shit.

FOUR DAYS LATER

FEBRUARY

'Engage-meant'

'Yes, I will, yes, yes'

'Tomorrow is our permanent address'

Wednesday 2nd February

18:45

From: Katherine King<kk44@hotmail.co.uk>
To: Seacombe<geobar22@hotmail.co.uk>
Subject: A change of mood

22,

Thank you for the quick chat this morning to boost my positivity. I'm pleased you are back safely in your little piece of heaven today. My GP came around to the house to do the same and made me feel much better. I have decided to eat a less restricted diet while on chemo because my body seems to be eating itself in the absence of calories. Still healthy eating but a bit more like your diet with lots of cheese! Seeing another foodie consultant in Bristol on Saturday with Tim. She may show me yet another path (hopefully one that's better tasting).

There will be decisions to make.

Don't forget our conversation; skiff camping on the Thames, dates and friends to join us in the summer.

I love you.

44 x

PS. Kiss me with words later?

Thursday 3rd February

10:45
Grey
Office forecast: ↑
44 forecast: ←→

K's received her second scan and blood test results this morning. She and Tim went to the hospital to go through it all with the oncology consultant. Her CA19-9 tumour marker is already over 170 compared to a normal reading of well below thirty. K is exceedingly depressed, as the only recommended treatment is more chemo that could, in theory, arrest the tumour's growth.

'The consultant is adamant that this is the best treatment for me,' she said. 'Tim is in agreement too. I'm so upset.'

I'm not sure what to do! Why, oh why did Tim – a GP – not diagnose K's 'hernia' last November. It could have changed everything.

I need to talk to someone – someone who can give me answers to all of this… horror.

14:30
An email from K. I must have sounded quite down when I spoke to her on the phone earlier, although I certainly didn't mean to be… not with her.

> To: Seacombe<geobar22@hotmail.co.uk>
> From: Katherine King<kk44@hotmail.co.uk>
> Subject: You
>
> I'm worried about you. You are in a dark place where

no one else can see the size of the burden you carry on your lovely shoulders. When I feel the weight of obstacles upon me, you tell me it will be all right, that we will be together, but we just don't know the how or the when. You are too brave in my brief company and it worries me that you feel you don't have anyone close to you who really hears what you are saying and is able to hold you, so you can express and exorcise emotion.

Do use your friends and family, please, to support you through this nightmare of Elm Street proportions (it's not a film either of us could bear to experience). No one can be expected to get through this on their own, and they will know how tough it is for you out there on the edge, unable to protect me from myself and from others, but managing brilliantly to protect me from your (di)stress.

Do you know what's under every stiff upper lip?

A quivering lower one!

You know it has been too strong for us to resist and I wonder for what purpose we ultimately are. Whatever it is that keeps you with me as I am now is a mystery to me (it's far easier for me to love you. I adore your healthy body and positive mind). You say you do not want anyone else and I believe you but still can't believe it. And I still can't believe I have given myself so readily, since no one else has been able to reach in and take all of me like you have.

I can only think it is because I trust you implicitly with my feelings and have done so instinctively since the beginning when you told me you felt the love that had eluded you for years. I, the expert in loving, knew nothing. You and I fit hand in glove. The way I feel when you hold me cannot be replicated, goodness knows I have tried in the name of duty but it just doesn't work. The smell of your clothes, skin, breath (especially your breath) the shape you have, your immenseness in comparison to my smaller frame. It all makes for an irresistible force that drives me to the next merging and will continue to do so as long as I live.

At first it must have been the alchemy, that invisible chemistry of scent and taste that made me desire you above another, and you declare you could do things to me that you wouldn't do with anyone else. I treasure those times in my mind and hope when I'm well again and smell like I used to that we can resume where we left off so abruptly before this horror spoilt a part of us not fully explored. But it is not this that held us together and I have been wrong to think you may be fickle enough to love or not love me on the basis of pure physicality. We have become the best of friends and I could sit quite happily in your company for the longest time, but that doesn't account for causing so much upset to others we left struggling in our wake either. We share the same dreams and do not overlook the simplicities of life that bring a happiness so often missed by those who have the means to afford the complexities. But it's far more than this…

For us to continue despite all the hurt we have caused others, to continue in the knowledge that it is the most difficult route to take and the longest way round. Surely in the grander scheme of things we are yet to be revealed.

Keep that faith…

44 x

Friday 4th February

11:15
Cold

K's father has just called me. It caught me slightly off guard!

During our conversation however, and while trying to justify my relationship with his daughter, I bring up the subject of divorce, but his tone is immediately reserved. He is adamant it is something I should not pursue or even think about now.

'There is no such thing as a quick or easy divorce. The lawyers will string it out as long as possible – they insist on making their money – and divorce is probably the most stressful thing anyone can go through in their lives, particularly where children are involved. Stress is something Katherine must not have added to her life in the condition she's in.'

I try to explain that K is already in a highly stressed environment living with Tim and that she only becomes completely de-stressed when she is with me, so it makes sense for her to be with me. But he is unmoved.

'Do you think Tim will make it easy? He will not let her go easily, despite what he may say from time to time. When it comes down to it, the realisation of what he is going to lose will hit him and it will represent a loss of control that is too much for a man with his inflated ego.'

Then he adds the *coup de grâce*.

'Have you ever tried to look after someone who is seriously ill? It is exhausting and emotionally draining, caring for someone who has a terminal disease like Katherine has.'

I try to stop him mid-sentence. 'Katherine is going to come through this, mark my words; she is exceptional. Exceptional, do you hear? She will defeat this disease – I know she can, and I'm going to do my utmost to ensure that happens. Do you understand? We are going to be together.'

I swiftly put the phone down and walk slowly upstairs to my bedroom, lie down, and start to cry. No one seems to be on our side. Everyone and everything are in opposition to the goal we so desperately desire; the simplicity of two hearts being alongside one another, together as one. As 2424.

But is this the price that must be paid when one finds one's true love? That, in the end, it is a forlorn hope? Can it be that one is only allowed to taste the ultimate fruit, but not actually consume it?

De facto: love-mediocrity rules!

Fuck Them All.

18:30

Calmed and equilibrium regained.

Have decided to surprise K with something, but I need her to be free for a morning or afternoon – and preferably on the afternoon of my birthday next week. I have somewhere very special to take her.

She will be at swimming tomorrow, so she tells me, even though Tim (and the doctors) have told her she can't go. We will have to see what happens, but I really want her to be with me next Tuesday.

Saturday 5th February

13:30
*Sunshine, cold +7°

K turned up at swimming today, just as she said she would. 'I told him I'm going and nothing, neither him nor this disease, is stopping me.'

She was in the water, participating, but elected to spend a great deal of time with the kickboard, floating.

Most of the other swimmers now know that K has cancer and they fall into two distinct camps: either they are (overly) solicitous, or they choose to ignore the subject entirely. Human nature, I suppose. There still seems to be a general denial about 'us', which is understandable – cancer and a *romantic entanglement* is probably too much information for any swim club member to process comfortably – but it would be nice to be able to be open about things with our swimming friends, about the two of us. Katherine and George, your swimming friends. Twogether…

In time.

22:40

To: Seacombe<geobar22@hotmail.co.uk>
From: Katherine King<kk44@hotmail.co.uk>
Subject: Watchet eyes

'Like two swimmers who love the water, their souls knit together without being sewn, no seam.'
(Rumi)

This morning you took your big towel from me as I lifted it out of your swimming bag and you started to dry my hair and then my face with the softest tendresse… all the while fixing me with your eyes. As I looked through those eyes and into my own I was lost inside you (the world dissolving) and left that place amazed and bewildered.

I realise how fragile I am, depending on you entirely to keep my head above water each day. You are a presence that never leaves me. A presence so real as this morning only imagined since then. I ache to be near you again, to be part of that heavenly dream.

Struggling to live in two worlds, I have lost my place. My place is to be inside your hand. Infinitely.

'Upon a bed of roses Love reclined,
The heart-dyed flowers across his mouth were thrown;
And both their sweets were in one breath combined,
As if they from the self-same bud had blown.
You could not tell, so sweetly were they blended,
Where swelled Love's crimson lip, nor where the rose-bloom ended.'
(Thomas Moore)

44 x

PS. I think I've managed to work it for your birthday! Have had to tell Tim a bit of a fib though… (don't ask!) Need to be back Tues pm. Please say yes. Need you to hold me all night and not let go…

22:45

<But don't you know, I do that every night… x>

THREE DAYS LATER

Wednesday 9th February

09:15
Sun, no clouds, good +4°

I will let K's email explain the past forty-eight hours. An *interregnum* I will savour the rest of my days.

> To: Seacombe<geobar22@hotmail.co.uk>
> From: Katherine King<kk44@hotmail.co.uk>
> Subject: Today I said yes!

When I close my eyes it is still Tuesday 8th February at 2.30pm. I am on a beach with a big bed of pebbles and curving shoreline.

Twenty-four hours ago, your left hand led my right upwards from the sea over a small bridge amongst trees joining the path that opened onto a grassy hill. We climbed to the gate and to the chapel door. Inside, wooden walls kept safe our world of quiet dreams and secrets. Unspeaking at the back, we sat with open hearts and an open book. Then at the altar, we stood beneath the small wooden cross, as if all those dear to us were there to share our special moment.

Thank you (my love).

I love you so much (you know this already).

44 x

PS. You and I. Tomorrow is our permanent address. (Cummings, of course!)

09:20

'Please explain to me this inseparable absurdity'
(Katherine King)

The inseparable absurdity of our relationship continues and is now sealed with our engagement. Yes! I have asked K to be by my side forever – and she has agreed. No ring, no witnesses, just one half of a smooth and shiny friendship stone that now sits securely in my trouser pocket, zipped and as close to my skin as possible. K's half is now tucked tightly in the side pocket of her purse, alongside our mobile phone.

I did not tell K where we were going – in fact, I just drove us straight to Ringstead Bay, only saying on the short drive down that there was something very important I had to show her and something important I wanted to do, but that I needed her with me!

K had no idea what to expect or what she was going to see. It involved a short and slightly twisty uphill hike along the coastal path towards White Nothe – a place that is our hallowed ground following the night under the stars a lifetime ago last August.

As we approached, I turned and said, 'This is somewhere that I think you will really like,' and led her to the small wooden gate and entrance to St Catherine's Chapel-by-the-Sea.

To call it a church or a chapel in the conventional sense would be overstating things; it consists of nothing more than a wooden shed with a badly sloping floor, a basic wooden altar, some chairs for a small congregation, and one large – but rather fabulous – engraved glass window by Simon Whistler. The raw simplicity of the place gives rise to its beauty. The simple timber-built construction and stunning clifftop view looking out across the sea has always powerfully appealed. When I first discovered St Catherine's I knew this little chapel to be something unique and that, one day, it would be a perfect venue for a very special occasion. Yesterday was *the special occasion.*

K was in awe, as I knew she would be. The quietness and solitude of the little place enchanted her, and, with an excited look on her face, she said, 'I can see why you brought me here. It's a piece of translocated heaven, isn't it?'

'I think I would like to be buried here. Out there in that little graveyard, with the perfect sea view. There can be no finer place to rest your bones. What do you think?'

'Yes, but only if I'm with you!'

'And that brings me to the reason I wanted you to come here today!'

'Oh, and what is it?'

I took K's left hand in mine.

'Come with me,' I said, and led her down the short, creaking aisle to stand in front of the unprepossessing altar.

'Marry me. Spend the rest of your life with me?'

'Yes. Yes, a thousand times, yes! Of course,' she cried.

'I am not thine. I am part of thee,' she then whispered.

We kissed in front of the altar, and with only the souls of the departed to bear witness to the absurdity, declared our lifelong engagement.

Thursday 10th February

08:20
F4-5, rain is back +5°
2424 forecast: Stage 1 now complete

Yesterday, I read a magazine article about the iconic song 'Ring of Fire' and country singer Johnny Cash. I hadn't known that the song had been written by June Carter, Cash's lifelong love, describing her existing marriage from which she was desperate to escape. It was an abusive relationship and her wedding ring became 'a ring of fire'.

I've never really listened to the lyrics properly before, but now, having read the story of its genesis, I can see how germane it is to our situation.

09:15
I have found a company on the internet, based near Leicester, that produces a plant-based extract they argue causes certain types of tumours – including those of the pancreas – to go into remission. I've checked some of the data on other research sites and it all seems to make sense. The thing is, though, this all-natural remedy is very new and unproven but is easy to take (as a drink).

They claim it does not interfere with chemo or other drugs. Anyway, I've spoken to one of the research scientists and he is happy to give us thirty minutes of his time. He would like to meet K and discuss her illness in more detail. I need to run the idea past K who can then run it past Tim. If he's in agreement, then maybe I can take K up next week.

Friday 11th February

06:50
F5-6, clouds +5°
Office forecast: ↑
44 forecast: ↑

<Tim said I can go???>

<With me?>

<It's worth going to speak with them he thinks. I can get child cover so yes next week! Another chemo again today wish me luck x>

<Am with you all the way x>

21:50
Email just in from K. It hasn't lifted me.

> To: Seacombe<geobar22@hotmail.co.uk>
> From: Katherine King<kk44@hotmail.co.uk>
> Subject: Friday downer

My mood is fickle. It sits patiently at a manageable level until elevated by you or when cycling through sunshine towards summers of yesterday. It then falls into a dark hopeless place and waits impatiently for a miracle. They do happen. I read about them all the time, but as it appears, in my ('tricky') case, to depend on a rare diet, expensive supplements, daily enemas and a daily dose of happiness, I'm finding it far from easy to make my way into the anecdotal case history books. Shamefully (because it involves negative thinking) it depresses me to think about our dreams of travel, training, sporting and social events. The rest of my life will be dominated by a restrictive and prescriptive routine of self-medication.

How can we be free bodies now? The absolute antipathy of what you want from a partner. My heart sinks. The alternative? As the fat woman in chemo, said today, on hearing of the location of my problem; 'Oh, you poor dear. My sister had the same. Tummy blew up like a balloon and they had to stick a drain in. She was four stone when she died.' She was considerate enough not to add 'in agony' but it was too late and I had added the words myself. I panicked and reached in my mind for the bottle of morphine lying in the kitchen cupboard at home. Made a mental note to ask Tim how much I would need, and to always keep a good Fleurie in the house to speed things up.

Have you really thought about the implications of tying yourself to me as I am now? As I will become, if the miracle doesn't happen? It would be cruel to help me leave this comfortable, if unfulfilled and at times unhappy life behind, if you were then to decide you wanted out. I can't imagine you would abandon me in the ugly face of slow death, but I would understand. Think about every eventuality, even bedpans and plastic sheets.

There is a certain amount of self-pity in loss, and I feel I have lost many things through this, including a healthy body with which to give and receive pleasure, as it were. I didn't have much confidence before, but now my flat chest (secondary to breastfeeding, advancing age and this weight loss I hasten to tell you… again) is the least of my problems. I now smell and taste all wrong and you certainly wouldn't want my tee-shirt under your pillow… But what if it never… I wouldn't catch you talking like this, would I. (No need for a question mark here!)

Yes, I am lucky in many ways and have been given a gift and all that. But sometimes I just want to moan about what a bugger it is and how much I want you to have the love of your life as you imagined she'd be. You deserve the best, the very best.

So, I shall get better for you and stop complaining (since for you, I am the best!)

Your Sweetheart…

44 x

PS. Don't ever stop calling me your Sweetheart. Ever!

Saturday 12th February

08:10
F4-5, clouds +9°
Exercise forecast: ↑
44 forecast: Not here

I'm at swimming and the word 'training' has been deleted. I'm in no mood to beat up and down the pool like a madman, nor wish to be competitive with anyone. If I could don a flowery shower hat and breaststroke widths, I'd much rather do that. All this physical energy buzzing about isn't what I need right now. I wasn't going to come along but K said last night that she would if she felt better and if Tim would let her go, but I'm guessing – listening to the pain in her voice – that her stomach is giving her more and more trouble and it's stopping her sleeping too.

08:20
I'm cruising at the back when friend John taps me on the shoulder at the turn.

'You alright, mate?' he asks. 'It's Katherine, isn't it? It really must be getting to you.'

I look at him through my steamed-up goggles and feel myself welling up. I'm unable to speak and can only nod.

'It's tough, but we're thinking of you, mate. Stay positive,' he says, before resuming his swim.

I feel a weight come off my shoulders. Just to have some recognition that K and I are an 'us' is such a relief.

This is the first time I've had any acknowledgement from our friends. I can't wait to tell K.

Monday 14th February

09:28
F4-5, rain is back +9°
44 forecast: By my side

Day trip to Leicester.

I am feeling anxious while I sit in my car outside K's house. Tim is indoors and I don't expect him to come out, but K is due to appear any moment. We agreed on a 09:30 pickup with instructions to return in plenty of time for children's story time. K has another chemo session very early tomorrow morning, so we can't be late back in any case.

I'm anxious for a couple of reasons. Firstly, being parked outside K's house feels awkward but is, I suppose, progress of sorts. Secondly, this 'sitting in a car outside a house' business reminds me too much of my childhood, when my dad would wait at the end of the drive on a Saturday morning, refusing to come to the front door in case he saw my mum.

09:35
Here she is now, but – oh, bloody hell, she looks fucking terrible.

K closes the front door and turns to walk across the drive, but it's unlike any walk I associate with her. She's bent at the waist and her right hand is resting on her stomach. Every step is clearly negotiated with concentration and pain avoidance. She looks dreadfully thin beneath her clothes. Her once gloriously shiny chestnut-brown hair now looks brittle and is thinning. What can have happened these past few days? The physical changes are dramatic.

I hold open the door and help her in. While she's smiling, pain is written over her face.

'Are you okay to travel?'

'I've just taken a bunch of painkillers which are yet to kick in but once they do, I'll be fine. I've got this bag, here, it's full of all sorts of pills I'm supposed to be taking throughout the day.'

'It's a few hours' drive, but we can make regular stops.'

'Okay.'

'In fact, on the way back, if you're feeling up to it, I thought we could drive through Henley and see my mum for tea?'

'Yes, I can't wait to meet your mum, just such a pity it's in these circumstances with me looking like death warmed up.'

'She knows I'm bringing you; she's baked a cake – a macrobiotic one I believe, no sugar.'

'That's nice. I struggle to eat anything now, but I'll certainly give it a go.'

11:35

K assures me that life at home is quite calm. Tim has been cooperative, and the children have rallied around helping out as best they can. Tim seems to be turning a blind eye to our communication. Thankfully our phone remains undiscovered; without it our lives would be unimaginably difficult.

K's had to give up work now and she can't drive as a consequence of painkillers.

12:30

We're sat in front of two white-coated scientists. A lot of what they are saying is going over my head, notwithstanding the hours spent on the internet. I scribble furiously. K's listening carefully and asking lots of questions. What they say makes sense, but can the seeds from a rare tree found only in the South American rainforest really have the ability to stymy the growth of a virulent tumour? With the situation as it is, what have we got to lose? We end up buying six weeks' worth of extract and burn a nice hole in the credit card in the process.

14:30

We're heading south, fast.

'You know my sister wants to meet you?' K says. 'I've discussed you again with Dad but have yet to talk things through with my mum.'

'Oh, right. It'll be good to meet your sister.'

'Neither of them has ever been a fan of Tim, so I think they will be very supportive when the time comes. But my mum is the trickier one as her concern is the welfare of the children. Who knows, maybe when I'm better all of this will be viewed differently. And perhaps attitudes will change when they see us together.'

'I'd like to think so, too. On the other side of this, who knows what opportunities will arise.'

'I can't continue with this half-life, it's not one I would wish for anyone. If I can get myself better, then new horizons will open up. I can see that now.'

'It would appear so. You're exceptional, so what's the problem?'

'Well, perhaps in your eyes – but anyway, these very expensive South American plant extracts may just be the thing I need and in six weeks I'll be looking back thinking, what was all the fuss about?'

We arrive at Henley-on-Thames – no Regatta this time, but we take a five-minute stroll along the towpath in silence. At a launch area for the rowing skiffs, K bends down by the water's edge. I hold her by the arm to steady her as she puts both her hands in the water, scoops and splashes it over her face – just like she did on our very first fate-sealing paddle in the harbour only last summer.

16:30

At tea.

It feels right to be able to share a central piece of my life with K. I feel an overwhelming sense of relief and a huge sense of pride. It's wonderful to be able to declare my love for this woman so freely. I'm so tired of living a secret life, and so is K. Any opportunity to tell people that we are a 'we' is to be grabbed.

I caught my mum looking at me quizzically a number of times. She can sense just how much K means to me.

As we leave, Mum gives K a small metal trinket and a handmade card, while I am loaded with the traditional bags of food for the freezer and snacks for the journey home.

K opens up her trinket on the drive back to reveal a small bright turquoise-blue stone and a hand-written note. 'Navajo Turquoise will help you to stay in a place of love and connectedness. This stone will help provide the feeling of unconditional love and connection to all that is.'

I can feel how happy K is as she reads it out. I feel it too. The words could not be more perfectly fashioned.

ONE DAY LATER

Wednesday 16th February

22:30
Exercise forecast: Slight improvement ↑
Work forecast: Could be better

It's been a long day for a number of reasons, and I'm about to hide under my duvet again when K sends me an email.

To: Seacombe<geobar22@hotmail.co.uk>
From: Katherine King<kk44@hotmail.co.uk>
Subject: A bedtime story for you

I dream that when you wake up, I'll be the first thing you see every morning. And you don't mind how shabby I have become because you and I have become REAL.

From the book *The Velveteen Rabbit* by Margery Williams.

"What is REAL?" asked the Rabbit one day, when they were lying side by side near the nursery fender, before Nana came to tidy the room. "Does it mean having things inside you that buzz inside and a stick out handle?"

"Real isn't how you're made," said the Skin Horse. "It's a thing that happens to you. When a child loves you for a long, long time, not just to play with, but REALLY loves you, then you become Real.

"Does it hurt?" asked the Rabbit.

"Sometimes," said the Skin Horse, for he was always truthful. "When you are Real you don't mind being hurt."

"Does it happen all at once, like being wound up," he asked, "or bit by bit?"

"It doesn't happen all at once," said the Skin Horse. "You become. It takes a long time. That's why it doesn't often happen to people who break easily, or who have sharp edges, or who have to be carefully kept. Generally, by the time you become Real, most of your hair has been loved off, and your eyes drop out and you get loose in the joints and very shabby. But these things don't matter at all, because once you are Real you can't be ugly, except to people who don't understand."

(I now know this to be true, you have proved it to me…)

Weeks passed, and the little Rabbit grew very old and shabby, but the Boy loved him just as much. He loved him so hard that he loved all his whiskers off, and the pink lining to his ears turned grey, and his brown spots faded. He even began to lose his shape, and he scarcely looked like a Rabbit any more, except to the Boy. To him he was always beautiful, and that was all the little Rabbit cared about. He didn't mind how he looked to other people, because the Nursery magic had made him Real, and when you are Real shabbiness doesn't matter.

I love you.
44 x

TWO WEEKS LATER

MARCH

'D-re-A-mi-N-g... I dream I will be the first thing you wake to every morning'

Sunday 6th March

05:29
I cannot sleep and have been pacing around the house much of the night. Have just checked my computer and clearly sleep is eluding K as well:

> To: Seacombe<geobar22@hotmail.co.uk>
> From: Katherine King<kk44@hotmail.co.uk>
> Subject: <no subject>
>
> 22,
>
> I love you very much and therefore I want to be everything to you. Being less than myself in physical terms may only be temporary but I have to overcome the belief that at the moment I'm not the woman you fell in love with. The problem is, my wants and needs are the same as they were when you earnt your medal and I wish with much regret that you had 'known' me then. I only see myself as diminished through the eyes of others and it is how they respond to me that determines, or perhaps reflects, how I feel about myself. I have found myself sliding back the lid from my lovely little wooden box you gave me, pulling out the piece of paper and rereading those words as a reminder to me who I once was.
>
> I hate being seen as a sick person – only vibrant and fit and healthy (and sexy) will do for my self-image. If I could disappear and come back to you as I was when you first saw me, I would, but things change and I have changed and to some extent things will never be as they were before.

For better or worse, that's the deal, isn't it? So, if you're in it for the ride, accept my insecurities as being part of the anger I hold for not being able to fulfil your needs in the way I thought I could. I am so angry, about many things, and it makes me want to push you away to punish myself for not leading the full and happy life I see in my mind's eye. It's far too easy for fear and anger to get the better of one's senses, as you know yourself.

Remember when I doubted you once (!) you said to test you? Give me a test you said. Well, I have tested you so many times, unintentionally, I should add, and you have always passed with flying colours, undaunted by my madness (where did that sensible woman go?) So take no bloody notice of what I say now my brain has been altered by drugs.

Stand by me. Stay with me. I'll make you happy. Sorry for being gloomy when you have your own gloom to deal with.

44 x

PS. *'The Blowers' Daughter'* is playing on the radio – and I can't reach to turn it off. It has me in tears, as it does you…

Monday 7th March

08:29
F4-5, clouds +9°

K's chemo finishes today and then it's back to the oncology department for another scan and discussion with her consultant, but judging by the amount of increased pain she's in, the weight loss and the bloated stomach and bowel issues, I need to prepare myself for bad news.

Tuesday 8th March

15:40
F4-5, clouds +9°
2424 forecast: ←→

Bollocks.

It's confirmed: the test results show K's white blood cell count is extremely low and her CA19-9 tumour marker has gone over 200, far worse than it was two weeks ago. The consultant now recommends she stops the current course of chemotherapy.

So, that's it. The NHS have nothing left in their arsenal; nothing that can provide any hope of remission, let alone a cure. From now on its palliative care, which amounts to glorified pain relief! All that is left is in the 'alternative world' and it's going to be down to herbal wonders, a variety of supplements, spiritual healers, lots of positive mental attitude, and love.

SEVEN DAYS LATER

Wednesday 16th March

20:50

Email from K this evening, the first for an age as she's been staying with her parents – a safe, stress-free haven.

To: Seacombe<geobar22@hotmail.co.uk>
From: Katherine King<kk44@hotmail.co.uk>
Subject: Back in Dorset

I'm back, but I have quickly lost my place and I am not sure where I belong anymore.

I wasn't looking forward to coming back because once I was at Mum and Dad's I felt at home, where I wanted to be. In the room upstairs, which used to be mine many years ago, a red rose in a vase, strongly scented. On the bedside table next to the single bed, a portable radio and small alarm clock reminded me of when Grandma used to stay with us and I added that book you spoke about – Touching the Void – a bottle each of water and morphine (just in case) and my 2am analgesic suppository! The bedside lamp gave the familiar room such a welcoming glow.

Mum and Dad had followed me in to check I had everything I needed and once reassured, left me in peace, and it was truly peaceful. The thought that I may be for once alone and in pain in the dark hours was only fleeting and didn't disturb the ease with which I fell asleep.

The five days passed too quickly but the calm and relaxation on offer was just what I needed. It would have been nice to have had an appetite, because I struggled to eat the food they had bought specially. I could only manage small pieces of chocolate and teaspoons of fruit pie and custard. Dad's mix of all things organic and wholegrain and Mum's green salads and vegetables went untouched.

In the bathroom mirror I saw pronounced bones leering through bruised skin. Emaciated was the word that announced itself unbidden. Since every set of scales tells a different story, I have no idea of my actual weight. My protruding stomach must account for a fair bit, although it has diminished since starting these damn steroids. I await the hamster face with trepidation, and even now feel the only people who will still love me through my ugliness will be my family.

My children and all my family were there with me on Saturday, including my sister who I kept close, exactly where I needed her to be. Luckily, I felt better than I had done; the day before I had been unable to do anything but lie on the sofa. The sun shone and we sat outside with coffee and freshly squeezed orange juice for me. Somehow the day passed all too swiftly even though we hardly moved at all. It was a day of laughter and talk. Mum and Dad wandered in and out providing us with anything we needed. My childhood friend Anne came to see me in the evening. I thought I might not want the intrusion, but in fact it was lovely and we arranged to meet again in the summer holidays, hopefully at her house if I can drive. It's a bitter blow not being able to drive.

Went for a CT scan and more blood tests this morning, results expected in a couple of days – I don't feel very confident though. Fingers crossed please.

Speak with you later.

44 x

PS. I have told them I have been in love with you since early last summer. Dad said he knew, but Mum was quite shocked! (Although she said she'd known it had not been good with Tim for quite some while.)

22:45

To: Seacombe<geobar22@hotmail.co.uk>
From: Katherine King<kk44@hotmail.co.uk>
Subject: Night note

Tonight, I stood in the doorway and watched my children in their beds as I'm sure all mothers do. Michael had climbed into Anna's bed and they have fallen asleep holding hands (just as we do). I wonder what must be going through their little heads? It doesn't bear thinking about.

44 x

Thursday 17th March

22:33

<Spoke with my sister this evening and she has offered her house to us! She and her husband are away for two weeks and has said we can use their seaside house any time we want. I know where the key is.>

<Fab. Let's go one day this week... somehow. x>

<Yes let's. x>

FOUR DAYS LATER

Monday 21st March

21:10
Blue sky, F-4 SW, +14°

Swanage sunshine and a day by the sea.

We are lying in the sunroom of our holiday house, overlooking Swanage Bay towards Ballard Point and Old Harry Rocks. We've spent most of the day being lazy, choosing not to wander among the boats on the shoreline as we had originally planned, but to save that for another day. The same with a ride on the steam railway. All too much effort.

Given the circumstances, we're contemplating giving Tim a proposal.

'What about we say to him that you stay with me for three days a week at my house and the other four at home with the children? That way you get a chunk of peaceful recovery time with me. What do you think?'

'He might go for it, but then he might say I'm deserting the children and my duties, or something typical like that. I wouldn't be, of course, but that's what he'll say. I can ask him.'

'He might say you cannot go away because you'll need medical help, but I'm sure we could cope. You are in far less pain – any pain – when you're with me, compared to when you're at home. Isn't that so?'

'Yes. I hardly need any painkillers when I'm with you – how wonderful is that! It has to be the love.'

'Let's put it to him, but why don't I ask him? I can meet him anywhere, any time. See what he says to me directly, face to face.'

'No! Don't do that. He reviles you! No, don't even think about it!

I need to ask him. I've had a lot of practice now – and anyway, if you ask, he'll only find ways to make me suffer later. Let me find the right time and I'll put it to him.'

'This is just so fucking ridiculous.'

'Yes, this is all so effing ridiculous, as you say. I just need to get better, and then this whole thing will be so much simpler.'

I squeeze K's hand and lift it to my lips. 'We will get you better. We will.'

TWO DAYS LATER

Wednesday 23rd March

14:30
Blue still, F-4 SW, +16°

Hearing her heaving pain-wracked sobs make me feel wretched as K cries endlessly on the phone. Tim's not going for it. He laid into her, demanding she stay at home with him. Full stop. No arguments. 'You're my wife and it's your place.'

16:00
I'm trying to stay calm.

16:45
Failing to.

17:49
I'm losing control of the situation. I have rage, a lot of rage. I am frightened by how violent my thoughts turn when I think of Tim. It is not how, or who, I want to be.

I am trying to be balanced about everything. Trying to be rational. I realise it is not all his fault. This disease is an unbearable corrupter of body and mind. It is pernicious in the way it undermines not only the health of the sufferer but distorts relationships, perturbing the orbits of those most affected.

I can only imagine what it must be like for him, to be in his situation: losing his wife to an intractable disease and then losing her again – to the arms of another man. It's enough to send anyone mad.

But if he could just find within himself a modicum of his nascent humility; recognise that letting go would be the right thing to do – to give K the healing space she so desperately needs, then the happiness that would result would surely be enough reward in its own right?

Friday 25th March

21:00
Blue sky, F1-2 SW, +14°
Work forecast: ↑
Everything else: ↓

Heard nothing from K throughout the day. She was not responding to texts or calls, but an email arrived just now.

> To: Seacombe<geobar22@hotmail.co.uk>
> From: Katherine King<kk44@hotmail.co.uk>
>
> Subject: Help!

I, having made my bed, should lie in it. You should not be led kicking and screaming into the nightmare that is my world. The taste of heaven is impossible to resist – but at what price?

It has been impossible to see you today without incurring the wrath of someone who can make my life extremely miserable. He has told me to keep him sweet because I need him, because no one else can look after me, and because no one else will provide for me. So, I have decided to prove I can do without him. I won't ask for anything and I shall manage any pain on my own. I will work out how much I cost, and if I'm too expensive I shall set up a charity for those of us living with cancer who wish to change their circumstances in order to live without it, thank you very much.

In the bath this evening I read a chapter of a book called *Love and Healing*. It came as no surprise to read love is '*ultimately related to health*'. When you're in love people say how well you look, it's something to do with the sparkle it gives the eye. Sensations familiar to everyone who has experienced the blushing, the butterflies, the palpitations. Love moves the flesh, there's no doubt about it. Unfortunately, when denied full expression and left unfulfilled or unrequited, love can be the cause of ill health (as when I am separated from you). '*All physical ailments reflect emotional and spiritual shortcomings*' (p.158). Tender loving care is well recognised as a valuable element of healing. '*Love melts away tumours*' or can do so in a healthful environment such as when we are anywhere together. But the amount of time spent in a healthful environment since January has been far too little, so how on earth can I be expected to get well? I know, you told me so. You repeatedly tell me so.

But when I am with you, I am at peace. Completed instead of depleted. With my body and soul at rest, I can heal myself with whatever it is that keeps me wanting you. Simple, but it is not that easy to turn my back on my family. And if I'm with you I won't let you go away. I shall cling on tightly and you will have to carry me as you did around the sun house on Monday. And never stop calling me 'Your Love'. Please, don't ever stop saying this.

If I could live in the little world inside my head life would be so much more enjoyable. Problems like ours take the fun out of waking up sometimes. It's a good job the sun is shining, but even then I manage to moan about not being on the (flat) sea in such clement conditions today, an ideal time for a novice paddler to practise her kayaking skills.

I do think about wimping out occasionally but would feel like such a failure. You must never let me slip. I rely on you to keep me from myself.

Can't let you or the children down!

I love you
44 x

TWO DAYS LATER

Monday 28th March

09:05
Some sunshine +10°

Just opened an email from K. She's *floored* me again.

> To: Seacombe<geobar22@hotmail.co.uk>
> From: Katherine King<kk44@hotmail.co.uk>
>
> Subject: D-re-A-mi-N-g… March in two years?

I nearly died. I was far too close to being only a collection of letters, photographs and memories – at forty-four years old, having always expected to live to twice that age at least, like Grandma. Not that I wish to be 103, just to be wizened and wrinkled and fit as a flea would do me nicely, thank you. To wake up free of pain every morning knowing my body is healthy is something I will never take for granted after everything I have been through.

I can't believe that only two summers ago I was struggling to walk, let alone train, although I did manage (stubbornly) to continue to swim in lane 1 even though I was far too slow. The others were very polite and never once complained that I was in the wrong lane, bless them. I remember feeling sorry for myself a lot of the time and had to be reminded to look ahead (to now) and turn adversity into opportunity to fight and focus on a future goal.

And one of my goals was to live life to the full with

Seacombe, as I do today. We never thought it would really happen, but it did. He has made a successful business and I make pocket money in comparison, giving the kind of support and advice I relied on a couple of years ago to stay in the land of the living. We don't really need my meagre wages, but I like to feel I can contribute to the cost of all the events that we take part in and the necessary gear that comes with any sport! I have a new boat now, although as fat and as slow as it is in comparison, my four-year-old beautiful forget-me-not blue kayak (a present for my forty-fourth birthday) still has pride of place in the shed and in my heart. I managed quite well with it in The Harbour Race to take first place in the women's fifteen-mile race. This year I aim to beat Seacombe in my new boat. Unlikely, but one has to aim high and I've come to learn that nothing is impossible!

I thought I would never have the courage to leave Tim, that Seacombe would never marry me and that I would never be free of the cancer that threatened to kill me. I will never use the word never again! I went into full remission a year ago and we are finally living our dream. Seacombe still works from home, so we see a lot of each other, which is important to both of us. We learnt a valuable lesson over those first two years of painful separation punctuated by a few snatched hours together. These days we are hardly out of one another's sight, except on the water when we often paddle off in different directions and at a different pace in the knowledge that we will meet up later with matching big grins and tales of sea waves and kingfishers, seals and sandy beaches.

We have not spent a night apart since February 9th when (in the small wooden chapel on the hill) he asked me to be his wife for real – rather than his woman. In fact, I don't know whether I could sleep without his arms around me now and often, as we lie side by side, hand in hand, I remember when I used to fight sleep and refuse to let go of him in the dark because I didn't want him to disappear behind closed eyes.

I love him as much now as I did in summer soon after we met. Falling in love happened almost immediately and could easily have been mistaken (and was by others who worried for my sanity) for temporary infatuation, a bit of excitement in an otherwise mediocre middle-aged life. But we proved them all wrong and I still get the same thrill of passion running through my veins three years on – when I catch sight of him from a distance, and when his eyes tell me he feels the same rush of love as I do hundreds of times each day. Our bodies have always been compelled to be connected and I love it when he can't help but push his fingers through mine, place a hand on my leg or on the back of my neck to steer me left or right. My shoulder fits with precision under the pit of his arm, as if we have been designed by nature to be together. All previous relationships, including my old marriage, pale in comparison and although there are times when we get cross with each other (which is normal for any couple sharing the same space), we are able to resolve any conflict in an adult way, which for me especially is a relief and a revelation. I think Tim realised before I did, that I had found a rare thing and that the love of my life was not going to desert me on the grounds of either morality or disease.

Fortunately, Tim has found his own happiness with a new partner and being the father he is has meant the inevitable cost of the cancer nightmare to the children's psychological health has been minimal. They are growing up to be bright, well-adjusted individuals with a great sense of fun and adventure. I can't believe we are on the verge of having two teenagers in the family! Michael will be twelve next month and Robert at fourteen already exceeds me in height. Both boys have the physiques of swimmers, a sport they love, although their nine-year-old sister surpasses them in her ability to perform well in competition. We have a strange arrangement in which we have kept the family home where the children live so it is easy for friends, school and town, and Tim and I come and go according to whose turn it is to be with them. Greenground is too small and too far away for them to live here regularly, and now Tim can live partly at his new partner's, it suits us as parents to move from house to house rather than the more conventional uprooting of the children every few days. When the house next door to Greenground becomes available we plan to buy it and knock through (the bookcase!). By then Robert will hopefully be driving and can choose when to come over. With more time and a double size garden as well as the allotment, we could almost be self-sufficient, in line with our simple, ecological approach to living.

When I say I will have more time, I wonder where it will actually come from. Our lives are not only kept busy with work and the children's activities, but with our own. Seacombe and I keep ourselves as fit as ever by swimming three times and paddling at least twice a week at the moment, plus running up and over the hill and cycling whenever we can. The knee operation has meant Seacombe can enter one or two triathlons with me this year – a busy year because we are also going on holiday to Sweden for two weeks to compete in a couple of kayak races, staying with a friend of mine in Stockholm in between events, and then we have the quadrathon which we did as part of two teams last year (women vs. men. Women won!) This year we are competing individually, so I am seriously worried! We wanted to do the Madeira Island race but couldn't fit it in this year (and we are still deciding on a colour scheme for the boat would you believe?) Closer to home, the annual pilgrimage to swim around Brownsea Island takes place as usual in August and we have once again requested numbers 22 and 44. Not to be missed the Henley Regatta, probably with friends in our skiff but as yet undecided, and nothing to do with sport but worth a mention, is our camping weekend under the stars in August. We have seen a glow worm every year so far and I shall keep my eyes cast down on the grassy verges in anticipation.

As winter draws in, we will turn our minds to skiing, a happy Christmas with the children and visiting our parents more often. I find I write and practise my calligraphy more willingly during the dark evenings when we are naturally less active and have produced my best work during the colder months. The book should be finished by next spring, and then, who knows?

44 x

10:00

<I am speechless! Keep the focus, keep the faith. We can do it. I love you Mrs 22 x>

16:45

I am drowning in tears.

I will forward the email to my mum. I have to. I know she will want to read it. But wouldn't it be nice to send it to K's parents, her sister? That would be something very special.

Perhaps in time.

17:00

Right then, K has outlined our goal; just got to make it happen now!

APRIL

'for whatever we lose (like a you or a me)
it's only ourselves we find in the sea'

FIVE DAYS LATER

Saturday 2nd April

08:57
Blue, F-2-3, +18°
Exercise outlook: Scrappin'
Wife forecast: ↑↓↑

At the swimming pool.

I'm shuffling towards the pool entrance, feet half in flip-flops, towel over one shoulder, and I'm already late for the start of the session. I shuffle faster when I happen to glance up as I near the glass atrium… and do a double take.

Is that Tim standing there? No, it can't be. Why would he be here now? Holy mother of God, yes, it bloody well is him.

Fuck, bloody fuck.

Standing very upright, arms folded, he is scowling.

My brain goes into hyper-drive. Retreat? No. Why would I want to retreat? Ignore him? No. Cannot ignore him. I've dreamt of this moment. Attack? A chance to attack. Yes! But, why would I want to do that? Yes, attack. That's what I want, to attack. Floor the bugger. No! Don't strike. Run! No, don't run. Stand. Stand and talk. Be reasonable. But what do I say? This is not how I planned it. Stop and talk. Remember what needs to be asked. Ask him to see sense. Ask him for us. For K and me. Ask him one question, the only question important right now. Approach, slow down, stop, be calm, prepare then ask. Ask straight out. 'Why won't you honour the wishes of your very ill wife? Why won't you?'

He hasn't moved.

My throat is excessively dry, I can feel it, and I try to clear it before I speak. But he gets in first.

'What *is it* that you've got?'

'I'm sorry, what?'

There's a brief silent pause, then,

'*Daddy, Daddy, Daddy*, I've found it. Oh, hello.'

It's Anna who has come bouncing into the atrium. She stands next to her father. 'I've found it, Daddy, the lady in there, she had my fleecy top for me,' she says, pointing to the office.

'Very good, darling, but now we must go.'

Tim takes Anna's hand brusquely and leads her away.

'Byeee,' Anna says chirpily as they pass me.

I stand for a moment, still dumbfounded. I realise I've not asked my question, *the question.* I cannot let this opportunity go. I may never get another. I have to ask. But can I ask him now? Can I? Like this? With Anna here? Out in the open?

Yes, I can.

So, I shout at the top of my voice.

'Why won't you honour the wishes of your very ill wife? Why won't you?'

He keeps on walking, his hand firmly in Anna's.

'Why won't you?' I demand, with greater urgency.

But there's no reply.

'Why won't you?'

Nothing.

I pace around in circles in frustration and thump the door frame.

Bollocks.

I think I've just blown it and there may never be another opportunity.

Tuesday 5th April

21:42
+16°

To: Seacombe<geobar22@hotmail.co.uk>
From: Katherine King<kk44@hotmail.co.uk>

Subject: More musings for the archives

I am here without you and in a melancholic mood. But strong. I'll not break as I did when I left you last time and those times I thought I couldn't bear to be out of your arms. Those nights, had morning been a key, I would have thrown it out of your window and told the moon to stop moving across the sky.

I knew when we met this morning that the week had been difficult for you too and that you had withdrawn from the world, but being in a similar place myself, I actually found time spent together in our troubles was the best thing for me. I hope I didn't bring you further down, today, when on the phone, I couldn't help but be a tad morose and sad. You must think like I do sometimes – I know you do with your quiet acceptance when I talk about it – that the chances are I'll not survive. My body is a constant reminder not only of the reality of what I have, something I used to be able to ignore and forget, at your house particularly, but also of the speed at which the 'alien' takes hold and sets a course of self-destruction. I do struggle to walk uphill but, can't believe the weakness in my legs and the overwhelming tiredness that saps energy I can't replace with food…

Sometimes I believe I can kick it, sometimes I don't, but always death lies next to me, at night when I am not protected by you, by at the very least holding your hand in the dark. That's why I need to cling to you, can't afford to let you go too far from me. I feel the distance when you let go far more than you do, and it's because I'm closer to death and to me, that means separation from you forever which is hardest to bear. Life goes on for others, for you, but I will cease to exist, miss out on all the world has to offer, all that I can give you, the children and others who mean so much to me. In the end I will be here with my family and you will be there and I won't be able to reach you. My big fear.

So touch me as much as you can and do, never pass an opportunity to be with me and tell me you love me whenever you feel it within you. It can never be too much.

And when I do surprise everyone and get better I will laugh at the things I write now and hope that you really mean what you say, because obstacles will no longer hold me back, I know exactly what I want… it's what's keeping me wanting to live so much today.

44 x

SIX DAYS LATER

Monday 13th April

09:55

Clouds, F3-4, +15°

The blood test results are back, so too are the new scans, and it is not good news. The tumour has grown significantly, almost doubling in size – which would explain why K has been in so much stomach pain of late.

'They have nothing left to offer me, only increasingly heavy doses of morphine. He even shrugged his shoulders. Tim has gone quiet and that worries me,' she said through tears.

09:59

> *<Have just spoken with the oncologist again in private. No one expects me to survive this – but you>*

10:40

Fuck, fuck all of this. I'm going paddling.

Tuesday 14th April

09:00

Clouds everywhere!

Am struggling to get out of bed as I can't see the point. I had planned to go swimming but can't figure out a good reason to make the effort. It hurts to even think about the pool – the place where I first saw the woman who has, through no fault of her own, entirely changed my life. Yesterday, for a few hours out on the waves, I felt less traumatised and somehow more positive, but it didn't last.

I spoke to my mum last night. Ever the realist, she said, 'Seacombe, you need to prepare yourself for the worst.'

I am not sure I have it in me.

Thursday 16th April

09:50

Fog

I've just had a phone call from K's sister. She spoke to Tim this morning after K took a turn for the worse during the night. Her GP came first thing and wants her to be admitted to the hospital's oncology ward. She has a fever and is in a lot of pain, which needs proper management, but K is stubbornly resisting and is insisting on staying at home.

Fuck.

I feel so helpless. I don't know what to do.

20:40

I so nearly didn't go swimming this evening but eventually decided I must do something, anything, so I am not sat here in the dark on my own. The session was pretty emotional, though. I think my face says it all, and the others could see it. I just ploughed up and down like so many times before, but the thought of K never being in the water again almost paralysed me.

Of course, afterwards a number of friends asked after K. I tried to sound optimistic, but I'm not sure I was particularly convincing.

I'm a mess.

Where has the colour gone?

When I got home I 'wrote' these:

Life Without

Los(s)t

it is so black and i am so lonely,
is this the man you chose – me only?
dribbling, staring – no things function
how much longer before our conjunction?

i am so morose, there is so much pain
no things satisfy – it's just rain, rain, rain
avoiding reality, no interference
i have no more, your perseverance.

i am too confused – it's all a big mess
there's no panacea – you must confess,
your hand, my hand that is all i need
you said 'Forever', now please take heed.

(dying is
so much
easier than
living
without).

Friday 17th April

20:40

To: Seacombe<geobar22@hotmail.co.uk>
From: Katherine King<kk44@hotmail.co.uk>
Subject: <no subject>

I have found it very hard not to hear from you today. In fact, I have found today so hard that it has taken every resource I have to stop myself from calling you to say 'help me' across the airwaves / microwaves or whatever Nokia use to deliver us from silence. I know you would make it all better in an instant, but what would it do to your day? You must be high on your work and I'd hate to bring you down from that. I am so weak and tired as well as uncomfortable that the mountain in front of me today is just to get up and move around.

Sometime in the middle of the night (a very starry night in August together on the cliff) from where I was lying by your side you scooped me up and planted me on top of you where my legs hugged each side and my head rested on your chest. I rose and fell with each breath you took and it felt as if I was moving up and down on sea waves. The smell of you was strong and I could feel your heart beating next to mine. You held on to me tightly with arms wrapped around my back and I was safe from everything that haunts me now. I never wanted to move again.

How do you do that? If I could replicate the sense of utter peace with anyone else, I would, to take the pressure off you a bit. But no one else will do. No one else can do. And that's why

I needed you so much today.

I wonder why it is that it just can't be replicated with anyone else?

I want to be with you, yet I can't be. I would hold you back and be dependent on you, especially at times like this when I don't feel up to much, but selfishly I want to be with you, at night, reassured by your twitchy muscles and on and off with the covers. I don't need anything but to lie atop you with your arms around me… every single night.

That's all I would ask.

44 x

Saturday 18th April

06:10

Wracked by insomnia and dark depression. I have been awake all night. Received another email. K has been up all night too.

To: Seacombe<geobar22@hotmail.co.uk>
From: Katherine King<kk44@hotmail.co.uk>
Subject: <no subject>

I am going outside now, at 2am, to bathe what is left of my naked body in the moonlight. I will wish on this full moon and make my promise to you again. When we go to St Catherine's Chapel-by-the-Sea once more, we shall seal the deal at the wooden cross with something that clings to me when you can't, and together make the life we have always dreamt of and talked about (endlessly, please, because it always excites me to imagine…)

And when you wake to read this, I will be facing my fear of what they are going to put me through at the hospital today, will it hurt me? What will they find? So, you must pick up that phone, face what will come and then go polish my blue boat to match the colour of your eyes.

I love you – truly, madly and very, very deeply.

44 x

16:15

To: Seacombe<geobar22@hotmail.co.uk>
From: Katherine King<kk44@hotmail.co.uk>

Subject: Woe is me

I have just seen my insides on a monitor. As I listened to the consultant explain the image and my (negligible) options, I grew cold and fearful; all my thoughts turned to you. How I wish we could decide on the next steps together.

My disease has spread. It is the tumour swelling that is causing my painful symptoms, which will come back, even though I am fine today. There are a couple of things the surgeon can do and one is to put in a stent. They are going to do it tomorrow afternoon under local anaesthetic.

I feel sick with envy of all sporty people. I want that to be me, us, doing those things, and here I am struggling to eat or walk, slouching around in a fog of tiredness not knowing when I'll see you or get in the boat for a good paddle again. It's awful.

I am so frightened. No one else is in this place with me. I am a prisoner of a condition that demands solitary confinement. My mind is sometimes strong but the evidence on the monitor represents an unforgiving unstoppable menace. We all know I'm dying. I'm not dead yet and I don't know for how much longer I will be here, but still the tide hasn't completely gone out. How long will you wait for me? I so want to wake and feel completely well. I want to feel well again. Get my legs back, my appetite, my fitness and my strength.

I want my old self back!

I want us.

44 x

18:40

Surrounding me is only blackness. I am at the bottom of a deep well, where it is cold and damp. The only light visible is one hundred feet above – a vague grey circle of translucent fading hope. I can hear voices from the top of the well, but they arouse no interest in me. My pain is too consuming; I see no purpose in anything. I am content to sit and stare. Please leave me be.

Sunday 19th April

18:09
Haze +15°

> *<Stent being fitted tonight! I may be groggy for a while but hopefully can be with you soon after x>*

Monday 20th April

19:30

K's sister has rung. K is home this evening – drugged up to the eyeballs, but the operation, according to Tim, went 'okay'. K is reasonably chirpy but very weak.

Clearly, there's no chance of me seeing her.

Tuesday 21st April

11:10
Not interested

Have been climbing the walls for the past twelve hours. No news and no texts from K. Have not been able get anything out of anyone. No one is answering their phones. Is she okay? Where is she? What's going on?

I don't know *what to do anymore.*

14:20
Finally.

<The stent has moved. Am in a bad way. Am exhausted by it all. Going back into hospital>

Later.

<Have been admitted to Ward 11. I may be here for a few days. Miss you, miss all the things we want to do. Sorry. Can't believe it>

17:40

<Everything has gone pear-shaped in my life, it's just awful now, far worse than before. I will text you as soon as I can. Tim happy enough because he knows I'm stuck here and can't be with you>

19:25

<Please save me. I wish we could have held hands and declared our love with a wooden cross and with people we love and with our boats on the shore... you know we are one, don't you? In another time and in another place, you know we would be together. We would be so happy together x>

20:23

<Going for a CT scan now. They think my gut is perforated. It will kill me if it is, and I don't have an option. I love you x>

20:25

<You are my English rose, my Mary Poppins, my bottlenose dolphin, my sweetheart, my true love, my other half, my... Everything x>

20:49

<Please tell your dear mum I love you and you would have married me, only me. Would mean everything to me. Please x>

21:50

<For whatever we lose...>

21:51

<...like a you or a me, it's only ourselves we find in the sea – 2424>

22:30

I have just received a call from K's sister. K passed away while in theatre this evening. Tim wanted me to know.

22:44

No! My world has gone. *How can I live?*

ONE DAY + MANY LATER

'Lost... in the ocean of grief'
'Depression is my only friend'

'And death I think is no parenthesis'
(E. E. Cummings)

'A love (and not of this world's doing)'
(Seacombe, August 2006)

Epilogue

And so, here I am, some nineteen years later, alive and still learning, gaining more insight and understanding of the *inseparable connection*.

And now, never ever far away. It transcends.

Bizarrely, what I have learnt is that through this deepest of loves, and through this greatest of traumas, neither of these extreme feelings exist alone – without the pendulum opposite. Neither can be felt without the other.

And I know it is important to have experienced this.

I was aware I was staying on a hamster wheel of going nowhere. Living in a world of memories, continuously holding onto the feeling of Katherine around me (though this of course, only highlighted she is no longer physically here and that constant pain of reoccurring loss was unmanageable). Seeking some form of pleasure to relieve my pain of loss was vapid and pointless. Depression became my only friend.

However…

What this voyage has taught me, and is teaching me, is that there is a higher perspective response, far removed – yet here and available, and deeper than the conventional linear-human-thinking. The bliss and love that continues to pulse through my veins from my twin, is not only that of Katherine – there is far more, much more, the other side, beyond the veil of this familiar known realm. She is a portal, a conduit to something much larger and much greater, one of Spirit – our souls Higher-Self, *the Divine* – the ultimate bliss state of pure peace, harmony and joy.

Heaven *on* Earth.

And it is a way of being that is important for all humanity to grasp – this *Divine Love* and to start living *as it* while here on Earth. For this is our birthright, it is within our makeup. To become the walking, talking expression of Divine Love here in this World, here now.

As Heaven *on* Earth.

How?

Well, it starts with the very basics!

A shift in individual consciousness, *read* – an acceptance of our own consciousness, raising emotional awareness, taking us away from hate and separateness and towards Love and Wholeness because… I am You, You are Me and We are All One.

And my next book, the story continues to expose and unravel the love connection and with help from others, this book will show, ways to a greater inner understanding and a deeper and rewarding outer new world experience.

Seacombe, 2025

Acknowledgements

I knew I had to write this story, even before Katherine's passing. We would often talk about it, joke about it even, because we both knew it was too incredible a story not to be told. Fortunately, much of it was documented as I kept every text message, every letter, every possible scribble of hers – and I had no idea why I was doing it, I just knew I *had to* for this love was so ferocious, so unreal, so driven.

We knew there was something in this, some greater calling. And once I began to discover and learn about Twin-Flame connections and all the powerful synchronicities involved, I knew this story had to be seen because… all people are seeking love and most are misguided, lost or blind as to what it really is, in its purest form. I know it and I can share it so, any guidance… may be beneficial.

It has been a tumultuous voyage to get this far and I would like to say a huge thank you to all those individuals over the years who directly or indirectly have supported and given me the strength to finally complete the story – *I AM YOU.*

Seacombe, 2025

Further reading

So, what is the purpose of a Twin-Flame union?

Twin-Flames offer a fast-track shift in consciousness to unity. It's a union created through the deepest, purest love, allowing that deep unfiltered love to be the teacher – to break open our hearts to other possibilities and to demonstrate to others, the importance of unconditional love. To ignite passion in others and to pursue *the values of love,* no matter what it takes.

(Annie Gedye, 2024)

For greater insight and understanding of soul and Twin-Flame connections, I highly recommend the following trusted reading:

Pradnya Pandit and her website https://awakenwithpradnyaa.com

Also on YouTube and Quora
Search for: 'On the Twin-Flame Journey'

Book Reading:
Only Love is Real: A Story of Soulmates Reunited by Dr Brian Weiss
Many Lives, Many Masters by Dr Brian Weiss
Reaching To Heaven by James van Praagh
Talking to Heaven by James Van Praagh

About the Author

My name is Seacombe and I live and breathe the countryside and coastline of Dorset and I love the water.

I have been a sports magazine editor and sports journalist for a number of years and writing has always been core to my work and interests.

The life altering, *I AM YOU*, is my first book.

www.seacombe2424.com